This book is for you if...

- You are worried about the future of our High Streets and the effect that the unchecked decay of our town and city centres is having on society today and on the communities of tomorrow.

- You've watched shop after shop putting up the shutters, yet wondered why no one in authority seems willing or able to do anything about it, or make credible plans for the future.

- You are prepared to take the debate over the future of our shopping experience a lot further than simply blaming supermarkets and big retailers, and into the reality of what the consumer really wants from their shops today.

- You are ready to challenge your own views on the death of our High Street and see the grim reality of the situation we now find ourselves in.

But, most of all, this book is for you if:

- You believe it is the time to do something decisive about our High Street.

Monotonous metropolis, Clone Town Britain, or Ghost Town Britain, call it what you like, the indisputable truth is British towns and cities are losing their identity and dying off. Independent stores that were once vital to the fabric of towns are disappearing at a rate of 50 shops a week. Some towns now have as many as 24 per cent of their shops shuttered. Boarded-up High Streets are already leading to a marked increase in crime and antisocial behaviour.

In recent years, campaigns have been galvanised to 'save the High Street'. It seems everyone has a view about how we can revamp our down-at-heel towns and cities.

But are they all missing the point?

Veteran retailer Bill Grimsey argues that it is already too late. The High Street is as good as dead already. There is no way it can be saved either, because the malaise has gone on for too long and runs far too deep. What's more we, the consumer, don't want or need it anymore in its current or past form.

The time has now come to work out what happened, learn lessons from our mistakes and find a new way forward to make new and innovative use of our shattered town centres.

In *Sold Out*, Bill Grimsey uses insight gained from 45 years in the forefront of retailing, at store giants, which include Tesco, Wickes, Iceland and Focus DIY, to expose the real reasons for the position we find ourselves in today. Ignoring the clichéd arguments, he highlights the crucial factors, which have never been explored before, to cast new light on the fatal erosion of our High Street. He also gives a frank assessment of what this all really means to the consumer and finds we have all got the shopping experience we deserve.

Most importantly, Bill Grimsey offers a practical and realistic vision for the future of the High Street, which can cater for the needs we really have today.

Sold Out will make uncomfortable reading, but if you are at all serious about making your High Street a better place, the solution starts here.

About the Author

Bill Grimsey began his retail career at the age of just 15 years old when he became a butcher's boy. His first managerial job was at Bishops Food Stores, where he rose to become a director, before joining Tesco in 1986 in the new role of customer services director.

In a varied and full retail career, Bill Grimsey went on to be chief executive of store groups both in the UK and abroad in South Africa and Hong Kong and has earned a reputation as a turnaround specialist. He gained particular attention for masterminding the recovery of DIY group Wickes, which had been at the centre of an accounting scandal that resulted in the suspension of its share price and the banks foreclosing.

Another of these recovery roles was during Bill Grimsey's four years at the helm of Iceland, which was renamed The Big Food Group, and was later bought out by Icelandic investors Baugur Group. Most recently, he worked with private equity backers heading the Focus DIY chain.

Bill Grimsey is an experienced public speaker.

Join the debate! Visit
www.vanishinghighstreet.com

SOLD OUT

Retail veteran lifts the lid on who killed the High Street. And it's not who you think.

By Bill Grimsey

Published by Filament Publishing Ltd
16, Croydon Road, Waddon,
Croydon, Surrey, CRO 4PA UK
Telephone +44 (0)20 8688 2598
Fax +44 (0)20 7183 7186
info@filamentpublishing.com
www.filamentpublishing.com

© Bill Grimsey 2012

Printed by IngramSpark

ISBN 978-1-908691-31-6

To my wife Jan, my mother Louie and my granddaughters,
Poppy-Mae and Violet

Acknowledgements

A huge thank you to all the people it has been my pleasure to work with during 45 years in retailing.

In particular thanks to David McGill for his patience and guidance in my early career and to Bill Hoskins, my partner over 15 years, for his support through some very difficult times with companies on the brink of failure. I have met thousands of impressive people over the years working in the shops and have enjoyed every minute of it.

Thank you to Michael Sandler and Andrew Hayes at Hudson Sandler for their belief and support. Also thank you to Chris Day at Filament Publishing for his creative input. A big thank you to Richard Hyman for encouraging me to contact Teena Lyons to start the project. Without Teena, the book would not have been launched; she has been fantastic.

Finally, thank you to my wife Jan, who has been my rock throughout a varied career with many ups and downs, but she has always been there providing her support.

Contents

Introduction

Retailing is in my blood and is the only career I have ever known. Indeed, my very first and fondest memories are about visiting the High Street and I am sure that is what fuelled my passion and instinct as a merchant. As a four-year-old in 1956 post-war Britain, I was growing up at a time when food rationing was still very much in everyone's memory and my mother Louie used to shop daily for food for the family. She had little choice because at that time refrigerators were only for the privileged few. Old pantry cupboards with air vents to the outside were commonplace in most houses and food would not keep for long.

Every day Louie and I would set out to walk the one mile to the short, yet thriving, High Street in Radlett, Hertfordshire. We would always begin our chores with a visit to the National Westminster Bank to deal with any deposits, withdrawals or bills. After that our journey together would really get going as we systematically visited each shop in turn to get our supplies.

The first stop, for example, was to visit "Winkle" Lamb, the fishmonger. He was a warm-hearted, plump, individual who always wore a smart navy blue and white apron and was sure to greet all his customers by name. The fish were neatly displayed on a marble slab which he would stand proudly behind while talking animatedly about his purchases that morning from the market. There were herrings in abundance, cod in great big stacks and fresh haddock alongside freshly smoked kippers. I used to gaze in wonder at his skill in cleaning, filleting and descaling the fish.

The next stop on our route was to visit Rodney Stevens, the butcher. The two huge men who worked there, known as Baz and Ron, also greeted Louie by her first name and always seemed genuinely pleased to see her. My abiding memories of that shop are of a floor covered in neatly swept, clean, straw-coloured, sawdust and the lingering smell of raw meat. I can also still picture clearly the huge blocks of wood with all sorts of knives, saws and cleavers which were behind the counter. Beyond that was a rail, which bore an amazing display of carcass meat, legs, shoulders and rolled cuts. Scattered amongst the hanging meat were fruits, which gave an incredible colour and vibrancy to the whole display. Even to my youthful mind, it really did seem as though the merchandise was jumping about and shouting; buy me!

Like most shops of the period, the person who served you would not handle the cash side of the transaction. They would simply hand the customer a piece of paper which would be dealt with elsewhere in the store, often by the storekeeper's wife. In the case of the butchers shop, a lady called Sylvia waited patiently in a tiny cupboard-like space for payment. The cupboard, with a hatch over the front, was illuminated by one naked light bulb, giving her face an eerie glow. Louie would go over to the hatch when she had got all the meat she needed and hand Sylvia the piece of paper. Sylvia would ask for the money, Louie would pay and the transaction would be completed with a smile.

The next shop, Freestones the bakers, was one of my favourites. The smell inside was unbelievable because all of the bread on display had been freshly baked in the bakery at the rear of the shop just hours before. Cakes of all shapes and sizes were also on display, each one more tempting than the next as they all jostled for position on silver trays. I always made sure I was on my very best behaviour here because experience told me that if I was really polite to any of the elderly ladies who served behind the counter, I might get rewarded with the gift of a bun from yesterday's display. The baker was meticulous about his produce, so everything that was cooked that day had to be sold that day. The only exception to this rule was yesterday's buns the store staff slipped to well-behaved children and the bags of these buns which were sold at the end of the counter for the knock-down, clearance price of a penny. As I got older I would often buy these penny bags on the way home from school and scoff them all on my way home.

The next stop for Louie and me was Hills, the greengrocer. Here, more than anywhere else, was when colour and freshness of displays came into their own. The people who worked in the shop were easy to spot; they all wore rubber gloves because the fruit and vegetables were so fresh they were often still covered in dirt. They would work tirelessly to creatively arrange each group of produce into a bright, colour-coordinated, oasis and then regularly top up the displays to maintain the vivid effect. Their attention to detail was breathtaking, yet the staff always took time to engage with all the customers too.

Our High Street journey usually ground to a halt when we reached Hills because Louie would chat to both staff and customers for what seemed like ages. I always found this a bit frustrating because I was desperate to get to the next shop, which was Wickins, the newsagents and tobacconist. This is where Louie would buy her cigarettes and, once a week, pay for the delivery of her newspaper that was brought to our house every morning before eight. Wickins had a delightfully heady smell of sweets and chocolate, mixed with fresh newsprint and tobacco. Lined up along the walls were an army of colourful sweet jars filled with all sorts of exotic concoctions. If I had been good and Louie was feeling flush, she might buy me a Jamboree Bag. This was a paper bag filled with mixed sweets with the added bonus of a small plastic toy inside. I can still remember the mouth-watering anticipation of being handed that bag and glancing at the picture of the boy scout on the front before tearing into the goodies within.

If I did get a Jamboree Bag, I was often a little impatient with the final two shops on our route because I would be keen to eat my sweets in peace. The penultimate stop was the International Stores, a grocery store that sold provisions such as bacon, cooked meats and cheeses. The outer window was taken up with a marvellous display predominantly consisting of pyramids of canned foods. In my more mischievous moments, I often wondered how many tins I would have to pull out from the bottom in order to make the whole lot collapse. Then, even if I was dying to get home with my Jamboree Bag, I used to love watching the man behind the bacon counter. His job was to slice the bacon using an enormous red machine. One of his hands would be turning a wheel at one end of the machine, while simultaneously the other hand deftly caught the sliced meat at the other end as it emerged from the turning blade. It really was poetry in motion and he never dropped a single slice.

The final stop before the walk home was the Post Office with its wonderful wood block flooring and solemn glass counters, where Louie would buy stamps for her letters and collect her family allowance.

The whole trip would take a couple of hours and, as I said, marked the moment I became hooked on shops and trading. There was not a second during the whole trip where all my senses were not alert or tingling with excitement. Everything about it was pure theatre.

Since then, of course, Radlett High Street has changed considerably, although it has not become as unrecognisable as many town centres today. If you go to Radlett today, perhaps half a dozen shops have closed and many more appear to be struggling to exist. The situation is, however, far worse in other towns and cities.

The indisputable fact is that the very fabric of our towns and cities is dying off. Independent stores that were once part of a vital hub are disappearing at a rate of 50 shops a week. Many of our once thriving High Streets are criss-crossed with unsightly brooding scars of boarded-up shops.

Retail vacancy rates, that is empty shops to you and me, are running at 15 per cent which means an awful lot of unsightly gaps in our High Streets. Plus, with some High Streets running with 'just' four per cent of vacancies, many of the big regional centres in the North and Midlands such as Derby, Liverpool and Leeds, have 20 per cent of their shops vacant.[1] In the Welsh towns of Holyhead and Milford Haven, 39 per cent of retail space is empty.[2]

Over the past few decades literally thousands of independent stores just like those of my childhood have disappeared. At the same time some of the UK's best known chain stores have vanished. In fact, there is a veritable A to Z of 'the disappeared', starting with Athena, Bejam, C&A, Dillons, right through to Unwins, Victoria Wine, Woolworths, YHA Adventure Shops and Zales. Many were, in their time, innovative and exciting, yet all died in the end.

It is hardly surprising that in recent years this rapid erosion of all our High Streets has really emerged as an issue and as each year passes and more chains sink into administration, the issues become increasingly more urgent.

---

[1] Local Data Company, Mid-Year Report 2009
[2] Experian, 2009

We are now in a position where pundits, campaigners, academics and the media are agonising over what is happening to our shops. Arguments rage about whether our supermarkets have become too powerful, prices are too high or too low, and whether we have too much or too little choice.

In the search for a 'baddie' to blame, the spotlight falls most frequently onto supermarket giants such as Tesco, Walmart, Sainsbury's and the like. Not content with dominating the market for groceries, with a powerful combination of giant out-of-town centres and High Street convenience chains such as Tesco Express and Sainsbury's Local, a strategy which has decimated the number of butchers, greengrocers and bakers in our towns, the supermarket chains now sell all the non-food things we used to buy on the High Street too. Books, clothes, homewares, electrical goods and toys can all be popped into your trolley with the weekly shop. The supermarkets are even honing in on specialist services and opening up opticians, dental surgeries and medical centres.

Whatever your view on this – that is convenient or downright destructive - what is clear is things are only going one way.

Widespread concern about what is happening to our High Streets has led to successive investigations and official reports in recent years. Supermarkets have borne the brunt of the criticism, but numerous other contributory factors have also been uncovered to try to explain the relentless downward spiral of decline. Top of the list are the growth in out-of-town shopping malls, crippling town centre parking charges, an outdated and often unfair property rental system and rapid technological developments which mean people can shop online, or even via their mobile phones.

The authorities behind these reports are unanimously agreed on one thing: we need to forget the idealised notion of the butcher, baker and candlestick maker of our High Street's past and to look forward to the High Street of the future. Indeed, the Government-backed Portas Report, which appeared in December 2011, urges the authorities to shelve all that has gone past and start again with a fresh sheet. The thinking is, we are no longer living in the same way as we did in the 1960s, so we should forget about all that and move on. The sixties are long gone, so they have nothing to offer, they say. If we want to save the High Street, we need a new approach.

With respect, these reports are all missing the point on a few levels.

Firstly, and perhaps most importantly, we cannot 'save' the High Street. Tragic though it is, the High Street is as good as dead already. Whatever we do and however we do it, our town centres will never be the same again. In fact, most High Streets of the future will be unrecognisable from your (and my) fond memories of times gone by. Believe it or not, many may not even have shops on them at all in years to come.

What we need to do now is to allow ourselves to imagine a High Street which is drastically different from the one we know today.

Paradoxically though, this means it is absolutely vital to understand and absorb lessons from the past, for until we know exactly what has happened both to the world of retailing and to consumers themselves, we are simply going to keep on repeating the same mistakes again and again. Whether we intend to or not, we will merely reinvent the High Street in a mirror image to before and, hardly surprisingly, it too will fail.

Which brings me to the second reason why the official reviews of our High Street collapse have thus far yielded no results of any note. We should not automatically dismiss and ignore the lessons of the past half century. While I am in total agreement that we will never revert to our idealised notion of quaint, picture book, town centres, I strongly believe that by drawing a veil over what has gone by, we are missing some vital clues in the quest for a High Street which will best serve future generations.

To me, one of the most glaring omissions in all the soul searching and chest-beating about what has happened to our shopping experience, is that retailers themselves have had very little to say. In fact, in all these reviews, retailers themselves have been conspicuous by their absence. Now, it may very well be that many of our nation's storekeepers are too busy surviving today to think about what may happen tomorrow, but it is my contention that those at the heart of our shopping industry have a lot to contribute when it comes to deciding what is best for the future. It is time to hear their side of the story.

Similarly, the one source which knows more about the motivations behind why you, the consumer, shops here or there, or somewhere else, and why you buy one product but not another, is the retailers themselves. Like it or not, the retail industry has been snooping around our store cupboards, freezers and wardrobes for decades. They have mountains of research into our attitudes to shopping and how we have changed over the years. This in turn has been used in a lengthy game of cat and mouse as consumer preferences change and retailers respond. The solutions they have come up with have not always been fair, or to the advantage of the High Street as a whole.

Be that as they may – the point is they have the information.

This is not a judgement as to whether either consumers or shopkeepers have got things right. In most cases they clearly haven't, but if we really want to know what has been happening and why, this has to be the place to start. It would be daft to throw the baby out with the bathwater when there are so many things to learn from the people closest to the issue.

This is why, as a retailer born and bred, I have decided to stick my head above the parapet in *Sold Out: Who killed the High Street? And it's not who you think.* My firm opinion is that it is time for someone who has been around for a while at the heart of retailing to share what they have learned over the years. It is from this viewpoint that I believe I am best-placed to offer some practical, well-informed, solutions as to what is feasible for the High Street of the future and to show you what is just pie in the sky.

I have spent more than 45 years in the retail business, starting off as a butcher's boy at the age of just 15 years old and then rising through the ranks to lead a number of the UK's biggest store groups. Along the way, I've been a director of Tesco, chief executive at DIY giant Wickes and frozen food group Iceland. I've also led international retailers in Hong Kong and South Africa.

In writing this book, I wanted to use what I have learned and seen in my long years in the senior echelons of retailing. Primarily, I wanted to highlight and explore the side of retailing that those outside of the industry never see. I also wanted to take the opportunity to travel the UK with the eyes and ears of a retailer to look behind the rhetoric and see what is really happening to our High streets.

Retail, as an industry, employs 2.9 million people in the UK, which equates to 11 per cent of the whole workforce. Obviously the majority work on the front line, stocking shelves, serving at the checkout and generally keeping things moving in the stores. There are, however, an unseen cast of tens of thousands at retail head offices who decide what we buy, for how much and when. Overseeing these people are the managers and directors at the top layer of retailing. This is, of course, where the real power lies and where we need to start the search for answers. It is my view that much of what has been going on at this level is firmly connected to the fatal erosion of the High Street.

In part one of *Sold Out: Who killed the High Street? And it's not who you think,* I will delve into the secretive world of retail head offices to reveal:

- How many major retailers have destroyed themselves from within. The autocratic and occasionally despotic leadership, which has been common to the sector, has put managers under intense pressure to produce short-term, unrealistic, results that have torn apart store chains one by one.

- How unrealistic financial and business models devised by bankers and retail entrepreneurs have destroyed the value of the High Street and led to hundreds of unnecessary casualties.

- How some of once successful retailers died because they spectacularly failed to move with the times and why they refused to keep up. It is a problem which still prevails today and will lead to many more store collapses.

This opening part will also show that the devastation we have seen so far, is only the beginning. It is now becoming obvious to those in the industry that retailers and property developers have also scored a spectacular own goal with out-of-town retail destinations. Many of these giant malls, so long the bogeyman for High Street campaigners, are now about to suffer the same fate as town centres and will disappear one by one because they have become secondary sites to even larger and more popular malls. The results will be even more catastrophic for UK PLC than the demise of the High Street.

Although, as I will show, retailers are in a great way culpable for the situation in which we find ourselves today, this is by no means the full picture. There is also the rather uncomfortable truth that you and me, as consumers, have played no small part. It is for this reason that I have devoted the second part of this book to a frank, no holds barred, assessment of whether we have got the shopping experience we deserve.

The truth is, our values have changed. The desire for personal service and customer-first courtesy enjoyed by Louie has been replaced by a demand for value-for-money. Getting the best quality possible, for the least amount of money, has had a massive influence on where, how and when we shop. Of course, if prices are lowered, that means there are sacrifices to be made in levels of staffing, service and environment. Yet, 'forget about the personal service, just give me a bargain', is apparently the battle cry of the modern shopper.

We cannot ignore the fact that over the past few decades there has been a massive shift in power between product suppliers, retailers and consumers. From the days when you could have any colour as long as it was black, we have got to a stage where we the consumer have real power to demand more choice, better value and lower prices. Or do we?

The fact is, like so many things in retail, nothing is ever as it first seems. Retailers have been understandably keen to try to retain the upper hand and have pulled out all the stops to make us all *think* we are getting our hearts desires. However, as I will show here, there is a gulf between what consumers think they are getting and what retailers are prepared to give them. The result? No one feels quite right about what they are getting, so they seek gratification on spending elsewhere such as the cinema or restaurants, and so the spiral continues.

The other reason why consumers may be increasingly less than enamoured with their shopping experience – and again more inclined to spend their money elsewhere – is that despite wanting choice, they are now getting less and less variety to chose from thanks to the current structure of the High Street. To make their models work, large chains stick to selling the biggest moving lines of any one sector. With specialist retailers all but gone, that means you and I now get to chose between the top 100 or so biggest-selling wines, the same amount of bestselling books and a handful of (well-known) DVDs. If you like something a bit different, there is nowhere else to go.

Any colour as long as it is black, anyone?

The pressure for lower prices and more variety has played a part in backing us all into a corner and we have ended up a million miles away from where we all want to be.

A lot of this will, of course, make uncomfortable reading but, unless we are brutally honest about where we are now, we have no hope of finding a way forward. Finding a way forward is clearly what we need to do, because I, like everyone else involved in this issue, whole-heartedly agree that doing nothing is not an option. If we just step back, retailers will continue to destroy themselves from within, while consumers will, albeit unwittingly, add to the downward spiral of decline.

Taking into account my knowledge of the retail industry, both in the UK and abroad, I have finished this book on as upbeat note as I can with some real practical solutions for the High Street of the future. It will be drastically different from the one we know today – and a million miles away from the one I ambled down with Louie more than half a century ago. There will be some shops left, although they will be very different from today and in some High Streets there will be no shops at all. I give my view as to how the better retailers will be able to survive and the changes they have to make in order to do so. I will also address the key role the consumer will have to play in the High Street of the future because we will all have to take our responsibilities seriously.

Finally, I have tried to offer some thoughts on how we could rethink the role of the High Street in keeping our communities together and imagined new ways they can be used as important social hubs offering opportunities for health, socialising and culture.

I truly believe that if we learn the lessons from the past – and of course don't repeat them – we can create a new, better, more relevant, High Street experience. It won't be anything like the one I remember so fondly from my childhood, but I am hopeful that if we work closely with the retail industry and involve them in planning for the future, we will be able to create new positive memories of the High Street for my grandchildren. It is a journey we all need to go on together and the sooner we get started the better.

PART ONE

Where it all went wrong

Chapter One
A crippling failure to move with the times

It is fashionable to blame supermarkets for the woes of the High Street, but arguably they simply responded to changes in demand quicker than the rest.

The first and arguably most important lesson I ever learned in retail is that you need to listen to what you are being told, learn quickly and never make the same mistake twice. Like most deeply ingrained knowledge, I gained mine the hard way.

I was a keen-as-mustard, part-time, butcher's boy at Bishops Food Stores, the supermarket in my Radlett hometown, and worked there every Friday night and through the whole day on Saturdays. I loved my job and, even though I was only 15 years old, already knew I wanted to work in retailing as a career. I couldn't get enough of the raw emotion and pride that went into running a shop. The sheer simplicity behind the art of putting goods out and selling them really appealed to all my senses.

Even at that tender age, I recognised that all retailers are essentially market traders who are dependent on the 'barrow' they wheel out every morning. If your barrow looks better than the one wheeled out by the guy next to you, then you will sell more produce that day. If your barrow doesn't look as good, your sales will go down. So, if you listen to your customer and understand what appeals to them, you were quids in. What could possibly be more satisfying than that?

I really looked up to the full-time butchers at Bishops, literally in the case of one of the most senior blokes, Chris Stockdale. He was so big, he used to block out the sun when he walked into a room and we used to joke that he didn't have hairs on his chest; he had twigs. Chris could be pretty intimidating, but he had a heart of gold and knew everything you needed to know about butchery.

I wasn't supposed to start until eight o'clock on Saturday mornings, but I always used to get there at 6.30 a.m. to join the full-time butchers in their preparations. It drove my mum Louie mad, but to me it was always the best time at Bishops. The store would be in complete darkness, except for bright lighting around the counter areas where the butchers would be busy building the displays for the day. There was a real buzz about these preparations and I wouldn't have missed it for the world.

On the morning I learned my big lesson, I had been sent out back to clean the butchers' blocks, which are the huge wooden blocks used to cut up and prepare the meat. It's important they look clean and I used to take great pride in getting my blocks almost white.

Using a bucket of water and a scrubbing brush, I worked away to make them gleam like new. I always found it such a satisfying job and like everything to do with my new trade, I took a real pride in the results.

As I was finishing up and preparing to go back into the counter area to start another job, Chris stepped outside to join me. I looked up expecting him to say something, perhaps some joke as was his way, but he was completely silent. He simply strode over to where I was squatting down cleaning the blocks, bent down and placed his huge hand in the bucket of water I had been using to clean them.

Then he just remained there, his hand dangling in the bucket and his mouth set in a grim, expressionless line.

After ten seconds or so, I started to feel a little uncomfortable. To me, this seemed like very strange behaviour and I didn't quite know how to react. Should I say something? Ask him if he was OK? What should I do?

The decision as to what to do next was then very rapidly taken away from me. Without saying a word, Chris pulled his hand out of the bucket, grabbed me round the shoulders and wrestled me down so I was lying flat out on the ground. With his sharp elbow firmly in my stomach, pinning me down on the damp floor, he pulled a piece of rope out of nowhere and began to bind my ankles together. Although I thrashed around and tried my utmost to get away, he utterly ignored my cries and flailing arms.

Before I knew it, the other butchers had stepped in to help and I was hoisted up by the rope around my ankles, so I was now dangling upside down. Still saying nothing, Chris began to walk towards the main refrigeration area. My white butcher's coat hung limply around my face, so I could only see snippets of the journey through the back room as I peered through the cloth. However, when I felt a shock of cold air my worst fears were realised. I was being taken into the huge, walk-in meat refrigerator. Sure enough, I was hung up, still upside down, on one of the sturdy S hooks, which were normally used for the large carcasses. With my heart hammering in my chest and my white coat still hanging across my line of sight, I could vaguely make out two large beef carcasses either side of me, like silent guards.

Then, for the first time since the brutal assault began, Chris spoke. "If I can leave my hand in the water, it is not hot enough," he said, his voice flat and emotionless.

Then, he walked out of the refrigerator, shutting the door behind him and snapping off the light. I was only left in the cold unit for a matter of minutes, but I can tell you now that it was one of the scariest few minutes of my life.

Of course, by today's standards (actually, any standards) this was a pretty brutal way to make a point. I'd certainly like to think that the treatment of young trainees has improved a bit. My point in relating my experience is to say that, distressing though it was, I learned a lesson that day which served me in great stead for my whole career. I don't mean that I always kept my cleaning water piping hot after that – although I certainly did – I mean I learned that I had to listen to what I was told by people who clearly knew better.

If there is a lesson to be learned, it is in your own interest to recognise it and act.

Throwing this insight forward to what I have subsequently seen and learned throughout my long retail career, this got me questioning whether a great deal of what has gone wrong on our High Streets is down to a crippling failure among some retailers to recognise important milestones and learn from them.

Could it be the case that many of the shops that have disappeared have done so because they did not move with the times?

Things change all the time and in the modern world the pace of change is breathtaking. In the 50-odd years since that shopping trip with Louie which I described in the introduction, Radlett High Street has changed so much as to be virtually unrecognisable.

Winkle Lamb, the fishmonger, which used to have that amazing array of haddock, cod and herrings, is now an opticians. Rodney Stevens' old butchers shop now plays host to piles of designer jeans instead of joints of beef and sides of pork. Freestones, that magnificent bakery, is currently a wine shop although it has recently been through several incarnations and was an upmarket fashion store up until a few months' back. The greengrocers next door is now a hospice shop, while Wickins, the sweetshop I loved so much, now sells fresh fruit juices.

The changes were subtle at first, hardly noticeable. The first stage of development came in the late fifties when a row of shops were built which bit into the green fields beyond. Architects had clearly taken great trouble to give them a 'village' feel, designing neat, homely, brick structures with slopping roofs. Bishops Food Stores, where I was to learn my trade, opened in Radlett at around this time, as did Woolworths and Boots. An electrical store, record shop and extra confectioner also arrived to fill the new space.

The next tranche of development came in the sixties and by that time the idea of keeping a village feel had clearly been dropped or quietly forgotten. The new block of shops was designed in a harsh-on-the-eye, square block style with no sloping roof to smooth its stark, unforgiving appearance. Bishops took the opportunity to move to a larger 4,000 square foot premises, tripling its former footprint, and Boots shuffled along too. The new development also attracted a new hairdressing salon, a china shop, a hardware store and another electrical shop.

In a matter of just over a decade, the number of shops in Radlett had quadrupled. This was all fine, because the population in and around Radlett was increasing steadily as more people moved to the affluent South East. For a long while there was enough business for everyone.

In recent years though, an interesting phenomenon has occurred. Shops don't seem to hang around too long which suggests that there is no longer enough business to go around and only the fittest will survive for very long. Indeed, the mix of shops on this High Street has changed every year over the past decade or so, with some shops staying for a few years and others gone in the blink of an eye. The most enduring recent resident is Pizza Express, which took over the site which the International Stores occupied in the sixties. Thanks to a high population of young families in the area, the Italian-style food chain has clocked up over 15 years in the same location. Countless other retailers don't seem to have got it quite right though and quickly move on.

Radlett is not alone in experiencing this phenomenon. In many ways too, it has been luckier than many other High Streets. Although many businesses come and go here, there are generally new ones eager to take their place and try their luck in the well-heeled neighbourhood. Even though there is a high turnover of storefronts, it is rare to see boarded-up shops for long.

However, in some other areas, this is not the case and it can take months, even years, to find new retailers willing to take on a shop lease. In some regions of the UK, mainly the Midlands and the North, it is not unusual to see dozens of boarded-up shops. Indeed, vacancy rates of 30 per cent have been recorded in Stockport, while Nottingham, Grimsby, Stockton, Wolverhampton, Blackburn, Walsall and Blackpool all have vacancy rates of over 25 per cent.[3] It doesn't look like it is going to get better any time soon either. According to government statistics, the number of town centre stores fell by almost 15,000 between 2000 and 2009 and the pace of shutdowns is accelerating. An average of nearly one in six shops now stands vacant.[4]

Over my career as a retailer, I have travelled the length and breadth of the UK as I have visited the various stores under my care and opened or closed ones from Aberdeen to Penzance. As well as witnessing new trends with my own eyes, I have also spoken extensively to shop-

[3] Local Data Company – Shop Vacancy Report 2011
[4] Department for Business, Innovation and Skills/Genecon and Partners (2011) *Understanding High Street Performance.*

workers who are at the forefront of my trade. It's thanks to this experience that I can say, with some authority, that I have seen some extraordinary changes over this time. I can attest that High Streets and shopping malls have changed so much as to be virtually unrecognisable and that those in the North of the UK have taken a particular hammering when it comes to an exodus from town centres.

My experience is not unique though. Although I have been in a fortunate position to get a countrywide view, everyone is able to relate examples of how the High Street in their own neighbourhood has changed over the years. There has not been a shopping centre in the land that has not been affected.

Whenever the topic comes up, which it frequently does now, the fashionable response to questions about why this has happened is: it is the supermarkets' fault. To a large extent, this is true. After all, it cannot be denied that supermarkets saw exponential growth over this period and if they grew it stands to reason that other chains suffered.

The bare facts are these:

Supermarkets have been around since the late 1800s and grew steadily in the first half of the twentieth century, but they did not seem to be a huge threat at first. Then, with perfect timing, around the middle of the century, one-by-one they began to adopt the self-service concept which was doing so well in America. (Coincidently, Tesco's first self-service supermarket opened in St Albans, just down the road from Radlett, in 1947.) Prior to this innovation, shop assistants would fetch goods for the customer and give them a bill to pay a cashier. Now the onus was on the customer.

The idea of self-service had not really caught on in Britain earlier, partly because the country was still in the grip of food rationing following Second World War. However, when rationing finally ended in 1954, everything was in place for the self-service concept to really take off.

Although supermarkets of the fifties were nothing like the vast hypermarkets we know today, consumers welcomed the development with open arms. The 2,000 square feet plus stores sold a range of merchandise in all the basic food groups, including meat, fruit and vegetables, plus basic household products, all under one roof. They were clean, simply laid out, goods were easy to find and the checkout process was relatively fast.

I can still vividly remember what my mother said when Bishops first opened its supermarket in Radlett in the early sixties.

"It is so wonderful," she cooed. "You can walk around and help yourself. There's music playing too!"

The supermarket revolution was, in these early days, very much confined to the High Street because most average families did not have access to a car. This meant that, even though Louie could buy everything under one roof, she was still restricted to what she could carry home. But, by the mid 1950s there were already three million cars on Britain's roads and the stage was set for the next big change – out-of-town superstores.

The conditions were perfect for large grocery concerns to flourish, and flourish they did. Tesco and Sainsbury's took the lead, but a number of new chains also emerged, including Safeway, Gateway and Fine Fare. By 1961, there were 572 supermarkets in Britain, but by 1969 that figure mushroomed to 3,400.

From that moment on, supermarkets have been relentlessly gobbling up market share. By the mid eighties the supermarkets' market share in groceries was 30 per cent. Ten years later, it was at 54 per cent. Another decade on and by 2006 the big four supermarkets control an astonishing 75 per cent.[5]

Today, believe it or not, the 8,000 supermarkets that cover the UK account for over 97 per cent of grocery sales and more than 76 per cent of groceries are sold by just the four biggest retailers.[6]

---

[5] OFT 838, report, 2006, Office of Fair Trading.
[6] Schoenborn A (2011) The Right to Retail: Can localism save Britain's small retailers? ResPublica

It's not just food and drink either. Supermarkets have been very effective at expanding their reach into non-food items such as books, clothes, DVDs, homewares and pharmaceuticals too. In fact, supermarkets now allocate more than one-third of their floor space to non-food sales.[7] Sainsbury's can even boast that it is the seventh largest fashion retailer by volume in the UK and Asda's ubiquitous George clothing brand overtook Marks & Spencer in 2009. Meanwhile, for every £10 spent on health and beauty products in the UK in 2011, about 50 pence of it went into Morrisons.[8]

Compare this to what has been happening on the High Street and the facts can make depressing reading. According to 2008 Competition Commission figures, the number of butchers has fallen from 40,000 to around 10,000 since the fifties, grocers have declined from 45,000 to 10,000 in the same period. Bakers have seen their numbers dwindle from 25,000 to less than 8,000, while fishmongers have lost around 8,000 of their number, down from 10,000 to just 2,000. And those numbers are still declining.[9]

If you look at this against the fact that in the second half of the last century the UK lost 100,000 small shops of varying types overall, it is not hard to make the link between the rise of the supermarkets and the death of the High Street. Smaller retailers simply could not compete against the might and power of the larger retailers.

However, it is too simplistic to only look at the issues affecting the High Street in these terms. No argument is this black and white. Although there is no denying that supermarkets have played a leading role, we need to know more. Before we can begin our quest to find out what to do next for our beleaguered High Streets, we must cover all the bases.

---

[7] Department for Business, Innovation and Skills/Genecon and Partners (2011) *Understanding High Street Performance.*
[8] Verdict (2011) UK Health and Beauty Retailers 2011
[9] Competition Commission (2008) The supply of groceries in the UK market investigation

We need to know what changed in our town centres, who or what caused the change, and which retailers responded the best. Part of this exercise will be to test the proposition of whether the High Street itself may be in some small way culpable for the situation it now finds itself in.

Is it that supermarkets were just quicker to respond to changes in society? Have retailers large and small been collectively guilty of a crippling failure to move with the times? Is this (at least partly) why we are seeing so many gaps up and down the length of our town centres?

In the first instance it may help to explore the major changes to the way we shop because over the past fifty years there have been significant alterations to our shopping experience.

These changes broadly fall into two categories. The first are ones which were instigated by well run, slick, retailers responding rapidly to changing demand. The second category is those changes which were the result of natural developments elsewhere in society, technology and wealth. Arguably it is the second group which may hold some answers as to whether the High Street failed to keep up because it presents what is essentially a level playing field. Everyone, regardless of size or status, had a chance to respond, even in a small way to these developments.

Those key developments which would have happened regardless of large store domination were:

1. Domestic technology

The prime reason Louie toiled down to Radlett High Street every day was that our family, like most others in the country, did not have a fridge, or much room to store produce. In the early fifties, just 15 per cent of the population owned a fridge and, even then, they were nothing like the huge contraptions you see today.

Food had to be bought fresh and consumed within hours. This, in turn, had a huge influence on shopping patterns. Clearly, as I have already shown, housewives tended to shop more frequently, buying small quantities of produce regularly. It also meant there were shopping 'bottlenecks' at two key points in the week; Friday night and throughout Saturday. Shops were closed on Sundays, so everyone dashed out at the last possible moment to buy everything they needed for the weekend and Monday morning. That was primarily why I secured my part-time job in Bishops, working on Fridays and Saturdays, to help out with the surge in demand.

Advances in domestic technology didn't happen overnight. Fridges were still considered a 'luxury' item throughout the fifties but the consumer boom of that era rapidly began to change the situation. Households could buy appliances like fridges and washing machines 'on tick' and they did. In droves. By 1962, 33 per cent of homes had a fridge and by 1971 that figure had more than doubled to 69 per cent.[10]

This did not transform shopping patterns overnight, but it played its part. Early fridges were still quite small, so it was possible to shop less frequently, but it was still nowhere near the bulk buying patterns we see today.

However, by the early seventies, the buzz of the daily trip to the High Street was all but over. For women, in particular, this held huge implications because if they did not have to fill their days with trips to get basic provisions, they were free to do other things. For many this meant getting a career, whilst those who chose to stay at home found better, more enjoyable, ways to spend their time.

2. Affluence, travel and immigration

The 1950s were a watershed for British culture, changing our views on pretty much everything. Suddenly, we were bombarded from all sides with a view of an entirely different world. In fact, we could even hop on a plane and visit those different worlds because the fifties marked the beginning of the package holiday revolution. Trips to Spain, Corsica and Sardinia were on offer, flights and accommodation included, for an affordable sum, thanks to cheap charter planes. Once there, our intrepid tourists could sample never-eaten-before delights such as pasta, avocado, paella and salad niçoise.

---

[10] www.retrowow.co.uk/social_history/britain_since_1948.php

Back at home, thanks to the deregulation of broadcasting which cleared the way for the introduction of commercial television in 1955, we were exposed to advertising pushing the latest luxury commodities. Cult American movies of the time painted an enticing picture of mass consumption, promising a rich desirable future if you only adopted the lifestyle of the happy families on the big screen.

Overnight, consumption became less about utilitarian needs and more about status and comfort. Suddenly, instead of eating, drinking and wearing warm clothes out of necessity, we became aware of the notion of 'lifestyle'.

Between the 1950s and 1960s the range of food products on offer in our shops expanded exponentially. Shelves were packed with new and exotic imports such as garlic, aubergines, pasta and different varieties of cheeses. I still remember my own surprise back then at the appearance of products such as coleslaw and rollmop herrings, even though they are nothing special today.

The growth of immigration in the UK has fuelled a great deal of these changes. This country has become a veritable cosmopolitan melting pot of different races and creeds since the Second World War and that has had a huge influence on our shopping environment, particularly the High Street, where there are now shops dedicated to goods from every nation from Bangladesh to Poland. Indeed, there is a strong argument to say that without this influx, our town centres would have disappeared a lot faster, because many of the immigrants who came in and opened these shops brought with them a different view of working and family life. They were prepared to live above their shops and take virtually no wage from them, to get these businesses off the ground. As a result, ethnic communities have made a huge contribution to perpetuate the High Street, which would otherwise be in more serious decline.

Another key date which marked another significant change in lifestyle was 1980, when Margaret Thatcher gave five million council house tenants the right to buy their homes through the Housing Act. Home ownership soared and the DIY revolution began. Before this time most tools and equipment came from High Street hardware stores, but now the big sheds began to appear offering more of that lifestyle alongside the nails and drills. One of the biggest selling items of that period were new front doors, as new homeowners sought to change the appearance of former council properties.

All of these changes to society presented huge opportunities to retailers large and small. It also presented a threat to those who were not fleet of foot.

Perhaps predictably, it was supermarkets and large chains who were the quickest to respond, helped in no small part by their scale and financial muscle. Yet, to tip the scales even more in their favour, the large chains went one step further by instigating their own developments which would alter our way of shopping forever.

These business inspired elements included:

1. Sunday Trading

In 1994 I was working in Hong Kong, running the Hutchinson Whampoa Park 'n' Shop supermarket chain, when the Sunday Trading laws changed in the UK. My view then was that it was a bad move, a sentiment I passed on to my old colleagues at Tesco, Lord MacLaurin (chairman) and John Gildersleeve (Director of Commercial and Trading), who dropped in to see me while they were out there shortly before the law changed.

"Why are you campaigning to open on a Sunday?" I asked. "I have to tell you, in Hong Kong we are open 364 days a year, with the only day closed being Chinese New Year and it is dreadful. There is never any downtime."

Their answer was simple.

Because there is a market there and at the moment people are going to small independents on a Sunday. Plus, it will shift the pressure from the stores on Friday night and Saturday.

Tesco was not the only retailer behind the powerful campaign to change the law. Pretty much all the other major and medium sized retailers, in both food and non-food, supported the change, bar Marks & Spencer and Waitrose. Sure enough, in 1994, the age-old Sunday Trading law was passed and the shopping experience in the UK changed forever.

Prior to 1994, shops were strictly limited in the hours they could open, thanks to the Shops Act of 1950. Over the years there had been 26 attempts to relax the laws which saw shops close at 5 p.m. most days, early on Wednesday to 'borrow' time to stay open longer on Thursday and then completely on Sundays. The various attempts to change the rules met stiff resistance from trades unions and religious groups. Margaret Thatcher tried and failed to quash the law, famously suffering her only parliamentary defeat in her lengthy term as prime minister, eight years before the Sunday Trading Act was finally passed.

The Sunday Trading Act was hugely significant because it helped create a new culture where shopping itself became an event and large retailers were quick to exploit it. After this, shopping began to emerge as a leisure pursuit and an activity for all to share. Those out-of-town destinations that could add in a restaurant or two and a cinema to the mix, were even better off because they could boast a complete experience. Once this happened it would only be a matter of time before a divide emerged between 'good' and 'bad' shopping areas. If your High Street was bland and boring, it did not stand a chance.

2. Logistics

The boom in the range and quantity of food and goods introduced in response to increasing affluence and travel would never have been possible without a step change in distribution of goods. Here supermarkets were pioneers and I will modestly confess to playing a key role too.

When I started out at Bishops, each supplier had its own delivery van. Throughout the day we'd get visits from the Wall's Meat van, the Mattessons Meat van, the Sunblessed bread van, the Wonderloaf bread van, the Eden Vale yoghurt van and so on. The line of deliveries was endless and I'd be dealing with one after the other. I'd have to keep my wits about me too, because the delivery men were a wily lot. They were real Del Boy Trotter characters, always trying to pull a fast one by keeping product back to sell on to independent retailers for cash. All the bread trays had to be lifted up, one after the other, to make sure there were not loaves missing from the middle. The weight of the meat had to be checked with care to make sure the van man hadn't slipped his thumb on the scale. The saying in store was; if you ever find an honest van salesman, shoot him before he goes bad!

This situation continued through the sixties, but as the desire for a wider range of foods grew it became increasingly chaotic. There was clearly a need for a solution to ease delivery congestion. To add to the sense of urgency, many supermarkets were waking up to the possibility of selling own-label goods, so they wouldn't be beholden to powerful suppliers. However, to do this, they would have to offer their own distribution service – something that was easier said than done when you are handling large quantities of temperature-controlled products.

By the early seventies, having progressed up the ranks in Bishops' chain to become a buyer and marketing manager, I was charged with writing a proposal of how to update the distribution system. My solution was a multi temperature distribution warehouse where suppliers' vehicles would all make their deliveries. Once the goods were there, they would be broken down into orders for specific stores and then delivered in temperature-controlled vehicles to the back door of individual stores. Each store got one lorry, with everything on it. My plan for Bishops was pioneering for its day, but within five years all the supermarket groups in the land had adopted a similar one. Virtually overnight, all the Del Boy van drivers disappeared.

The modernisation of distribution paved the way for even larger ranges and varieties in store.

3. Resale Price Maintenance

Walk down the High Street today, or surf the Internet and everything is about price, price, price. The search for a bargain (and its acquisition) is part of the pleasure of the shopping experience. It was not always so.

In the early fifties, most ordinary people did not think about the cost of goods too much. It was what it was. Most of the time it was just a relief to be able to afford basic goods.

The reason why price had not yet become an issue was: Resale Price Maintenance (RPM).

RPM was the impediment to the highly competitive price-led business model we know today and was the practice whereby a manufacturer and its distributors agreed the price at which goods would be sold. Any retailer that tried to undercut this cosy arrangement would swiftly find their supply abruptly cut off.

The idea behind RPM was to protect small stores from unfair competition from larger retailers, which could discount goods thanks to their economies of scale. It also worked out very nicely for manufacturers too, because, if larger retailers discounted their prices, it would almost certainly drive down profits for the company that produced the product.

Opponents of RPM became increasingly vocal throughout the last century progressed, not least Jack Cohen, who founded Tesco in 1919. An innovative retailer, Cohen was building up a substantial empire of grocery shops based on the premise of 'a good deal'.

By 1956, thanks to sustained and highly vocal lobbying, the scope of RPM was reduced considerably but this was still not enough for its detractors. In early 1961, Cohen stepped up his campaign to get rid of it altogether. By this time Tesco, now with more than 185 stores, had just opened its largest most comprehensive store yet, a flagship shop in Leicester which offered a restaurant, a car wash, a filling station and a Home 'n' Wear station selling good value clothes.

In an early example of the potential of supermarket power, the authorities quickly capitulated. In 1964, the Resale Prices Act declared all resale price agreements to be against the public interest.

Although the repercussions of the abolition of RPM were breathtakingly quick and supermarkets exponentially increased their market share, the most hard-hitting result of this move was still a few years away. Checkout 77, which came about as a direct result of the abolition of RPM, would change the face of retailing and the High Street forever.

4. Checkout 77

The 1970s was the era of rampant inflation. It averaged 13 per cent over the decade and peaked at a whopping 25 per cent in 1975. Shops didn't even have to open their doors to be making money on their balance sheets because all they had to do was revalue their stock.

Ian MacLaurin, who took over from Jack Cohen in 1973, didn't just sit back and do nothing though. He saw it as a huge opportunity for Tesco to strike a serious blow against its rivals. MacLaurin's plan was to step away from the model of living hand-to-mouth on tiny margins as a pile it high retailer, and become an aspirational mass retailer. To do this, Tesco needed scale and MacLaurin's gaze fell upon Green Shield Stamps, the ubiquitous trading stamps which had been offered by his store since 1963 and by many other High Street chains besides.

His view was: did the consumer really care about collecting stamps for tiny rewards, when inflation was in double figures? Or would they prefer lower prices?

In 1977, in a bold move, MacLaurin ditched the stamps. He used the £20 million saved by this to finance price reductions and a massive TV campaign extolling the virtues of Checkout 77.

"Checkout our prices!" screamed the adverts.

Tesco's market share went from seven per cent to 14 per cent almost overnight.

This leap in growth had huge implications on Tesco's infrastructure, which took time to resolve. It also did not go unheeded by rivals who scrambled to catch up — Sainsbury's for example responded with Discount 78 the following year.

However, the point was, Tesco had moved first and crucially set the ball rolling that price and scale were important.

After this, there was no going back.

What does all of this tell us? It shows that, whether they instigated the change, or merely spotted that it was happening, supermarkets in particular have never been slow to react. Going back to the lesson which opened this chapter, they didn't need telling twice. The supermarket success story of modern times is based on the fact that if things were going in one direction, they'd always step up to the plate to meet the new challenge.

It wasn't always easy either. As I showed earlier, the surge in demand following Checkout 77 really did catch Tesco out. For a while it suffered from empty, unstocked, shelves, which is the worst nightmare for any retailer. It simply could not replenish them quick enough. However, the chain immediately reacted. MacLaurin realised the distribution side needed fixing and invested heavily in new distribution centres around the country which were built up in months.

The key developments listed here were just the tip of the iceberg too. Time and again, supermarkets and large chains have spotted a trend and ruthlessly done all they could to keep ahead of it. Bumping along OK was never an option.

Take technology for example. At this time all the major supermarket chains reinvested large sums of money in technology to speed things up all the way down the line. When I first started out, we used to do our price changes manually. There was a sheet of paper called a 'flimsy' with the products listed down one side, with the old prices and new prices in a column beside it. I'd literally have to cross out one price and then send it down to the computer department so they could key it in on these massive machines. One week later I'd get a sheet of paper back that I would have to check with a fine toothcomb to make sure we had been charged the right price. This clearly would not do if the large stores were to make instant, eye-catching, new price cuts, so a faster, more efficient method was found.

It didn't stop here either. The advances in technology and logistics paved the way for the building of larger stores selling a bigger range of goods. Happily for the supermarkets and DIY sheds, UK planning rules were gradually relaxed in the 1970s and 1980s, which allowed them to build large supermarkets outside of town centres. (We will discuss this in more detail later in this book.) Plus, growing car ownership meant people were happy to drive to these vast new stores. The major retailers, of course, left nothing to chance and I still remember in my early days at Tesco when I was opening 20 new superstores a year as the new store development director, an important part of this undertaking was to offer townsfolk nearby a free bus service to the new store.

So, the obvious response is; what was the rest of the High Street doing during this time? Did individual retailers fight back? Did they find a way to keep Louie off the bus to Tesco? Was it even possible to stop the march of progress?

With the benefit of hindsight, it is easy to see that supermarkets and some larger retailers were much better at reading the signs and moving with the times. It probably helped that they began with a certain amount of scale to begin with, but what you cannot escape is the fact that they were led by some pretty savvy business leaders such as Jack Cohen and Ian MacLaurin and latterly by Sir Terry Leahy who took Tesco global.

However, there is also evidence that at least some of the stores that failed did so because they didn't keep up. They got to a certain size and sat back on their laurels. Before long the world passed them by. The result of this complacency was usually fatal.

One of the most interesting examples of this is one-time High Street favourite Woolworths. Although almost identical to rival variety chain Wilkinson, Woolies is no more, while Wilkinson thrives. If you stuck to the argument that supermarkets have driven variety stores off the market, surely both would have disappeared into the retail history books? This is clearly not the case, so you cannot help but surmise that Woolworths did something very wrong.

Once again, let's look at the available facts.

In December 2008, just weeks before what was supposed to be its centenary celebration, Woolworths went into administration. The collapse of the variety store retailer put 30,000 people out of work and shutters were put up on more than 800 stores. Meanwhile, the privately owned Wilkinson chain which has a pretty much identical offering to Woolworths, continues to go from strength to strength with a turnover in excess of £1.5 billion, profits of more than £61 million, plus over 335 stores and growing[11].

Both chains sold similar products, from similar sized stores in similar locations. Why did one succeed, yet the other fail?

Woolworths could claim to have been dealt a very bad hand by its one-time parent company Kingfisher. Hundreds of its stores were let on pretty dreadful terms, not least 182 shops that were sold by Kingfisher just days before the break-up of the group in 2001. That sale and lease back raised a respectable £614 million[12] for Kingfisher, but saddled Woolworths with 25-year leases with a minimum annual rent increase of 2.5 per cent a year[13].

But, there was more to Woolworths' problems than swingeing rent increases. The stores had lost their way long before the break-up of Kingfisher.

In the eighties, in a bid to stay competitive, Woolworths looked at its costs and decided the way forward was to cut back on some of the layers in its managerial staff. Now, in retailing you have many disciplines, such as store operations, logistics, buying, marketing, finance and so on. If you want to have any sort of success as a retailer of any scale, you need to keep a careful eye on all these elements. In years gone by, Woolworths had even gone one step further by employing 'superintendents' to make sure standards were maintained in every discipline. These guys were suited and booted, with eyes so keen they could spot a missing price tag at 20 yards.

When the cost cuts of the eighties came in, the first thing to go were the superintendents, along with many other crucial elements of the pyramid structure. Standards quickly began to slip. In a matter of years, the stores became more of a market bazaar than a fully functioning

[11] http://corporate.wilkinsonplus.com
[12] Retail Week
[13] Retail Week

professional retailer. Worse still, the units became increasingly dirty and unkempt. I well remember a marketing executive telling me about a management trip around the stores where the team had to visit 18 shops before they found one where the 'W' of the Woolworth sign on the front of the shop was actually intact!

So, at the very time when consumers were becoming more worldly-wise and affluent and used to the slick, clean operations of supermarkets, Woolworths were offering them something way below par. There was little interest in the changing needs of the modern shopper, indeed it seemed to have played no part in this store's planning whatsoever.

To make things worse – no one did anything about it. With the arrogance of a shop that had always been the number one confectionery seller in the country, they expected it to be ever thus. The long-held belief was that the customer would get what they were given. No one questioned why they were haemorrhaging market share until the chain had drifted to a point where it was too late to save.

Contrast this with Wilkinson, the rival variety chain, which has gone from strength to strength and has carved out a decent niche in the modern market. Wilkinson has built its brand by copying the supermarket model. (Copying is just fine – what is important is to move with the times.) The stores are clean, uncluttered and the goods are easy to find. The business model is lean – they carry less stock and rely on just-in-time deliveries. Plus, although management numbers are kept deliberately low, they zealously tick all the boxes on the various elements of retailing that needed to be followed.

If you look back through the history of modern retailing, there have been plenty of retailers which have lost their way and failed to adapt. Most of the time, there is very little that can be done once they reach a certain point and the next step is for them to fall into administration and disappear from the High Street. On some rare occasions it is possible to halt the decline and refresh a brand for the modern era. The most notable example of this was the reinvention of Marks & Spencer by Sir Stuart Rose between 2004 and 2010.

In the 1990s, M&S, the former High Street darling, suffered a horrific downturn as shoppers rejected it and took their money elsewhere. The chain was uncompetitive on price and the products and stores were viewed as dowdy and unfashionable. Other new kids on the block, such as Zara and H&M, were seen to be more in tune with what shoppers wanted from their clothes stores. Customers were being easily lured away by cheaper, snazzier and more aggressive rivals.

Sir Stuart's solution was not rocket science – although no one else seemed to have thought of it. He simply brought the customer back to the forefront and went about widening the brand's appeal from functional to fashionable which appealed to all ages and both genders. Then, he set it off with a very clever marketing campaign bringing in celebrities such as sixties favourite Twiggy, supermodel Erin O'Connor and TV personality Myleene Klass to appeal to their respective age groups. It worked and he managed to reverse the dwindling fortunes of the chain and dramatically slow the decline.

At the other end of the scale, consider mobile phone chains, such as Carphone Warehouse and Phones4U. These stores came out of nowhere, spotted the potential of a technology that was in its infancy and presented it in a way the customer wanted.

What does all this show us? It shows that retailers have to be alert to what consumers want and most of all, customers want convenience and ways to save time on tedious tasks. Convenience has driven the market.

If you look back through the last 50 years there have been some dramatic changes in society, technology and wealth. Shops which have recognised these changes and moved with them to make the shopper experience a faster, easier and more pleasant experience have done well. Those which have failed to keep up have died.

Perhaps the biggest lesson of all is while it is essential to heed our lessons, there is no use harping back to the past as the model for a future High Street. There is no point trying to recreate the conditions which Louie encountered when she used to do her daily shop. She, like everyone else, no longer requires this. There is no point recreating the past.

Everyone has grown accustomed to getting into their car, driving to a large superstore and buying all that they need for the week, or even fortnight, ahead. They don't need a quaint High Street with a fishmonger, a butcher, a bakery and a hardware store.

They would very rarely use it.

What retailers need to do now is to work out what consumers will need in the future so that those who are still around can survive and thrive in modern times. That means accepting that people covet their free time, so any shop that can help them save it will be quids in.

Most importantly, all the significant changes that have been highlighted here are not the last of it. Whether or not the new developments are instigated by society, academics or retail giants, can you imagine what might happen in the next half century? If you are a retailer, you should certainly be trying. Online retailing, is just on example. It is already the fastest growing competitor to bricks and mortar retailing, and Internet sales have doubled from 5.1 per cent of total retail sales in 2000 to 10.2 per cent in 2011. It is expected to rise to 12.2 per cent by 2014.[14] If anything, this may even be an underestimate of online's potential according to OFCOM. Almost 80 per cent of UK Internet users said they ordered online in 2010.

But, there are plenty of other developments to keep an eye on too. It is only a matter of time, for example, before money is pretty much gone altogether and we are all paying for our goods with a swipe of our mobile phones.

I've always imagined that we will one day be able to shop by wearing a pair of high-tech glasses which will enable you to 'walk' down virtual aisles in the comfort of your own home. Look at a product you like and zap, it is in your trolley and winging its way to you. The way technology is progressing, this is not such an unbelievable flight of fancy.

---

[14] Verdict

When I worked for Tesco, Ian MacLaurin used to put all of his executives into teams and would charge each group with thinking about a particular scenario ten years ahead. Then, that team would have to present its ideas to the rest of the senior executives on an away weekend. The stuff we all came up with was amazingly powerful and paved the way for a lot of the strategy going forward. I've no reason not to believe that they, and other top retailers, still do the same sort of thing today.

How many other retailers are thinking about things in these terms though? How about the government, or town councils? The changes we have seen over the past 50 years will be matched by equally monumental steps forward in the next half century. They may well be even more far-reaching than anything that has gone before.

Now is the time to learn from the past and start planning ahead.

Chapter Two
A problem that begins from within

Retail, as a sector, is an entertaining place to work, but can outdated management techniques have sometimes hindered its progress?

R etail, as an industry, has always attracted its fair share of larger-than-life characters. It's a business that requires a unique combination of creativity, business acumen, negotiation skills and more than a little bit of chutzpah. Many of the nation's most successful shopkeepers seem to be those who sail as close as possible to the wind without getting blown off course completely.

Unfortunately, as I once discovered when I met one of the most powerful people on the British High Street, this often means that none of the normal rules seem to apply, which can be to the detriment of those on the receiving end. The person I am referring to is Sir Philip Green, the billionaire fashion tycoon who owns the Arcadia Group, which includes chains such as BHS, Topshop, Dorothy Perkins and Miss Selfridge.

The first and last time I met Sir Philip was in the year 2002, back then he was just plain Philip Green because he was not knighted until 2006. It would be fair to say that both of us had had a busy time over the preceding year. I had joined the frozen food group Iceland in January, fresh from fighting a takeover bid at Wickes, my previous firm. Just weeks after joining, Malcolm Walker, Iceland's co-founder and chairman, had left abruptly just after the chain had issued a severe profit warning. In the weeks that followed, we issued two further profits warnings as I struggled to get Iceland back on track.

In the same year, Green had abandoned his contentious bid for Marks & Spencer and bought department store chain BHS for £200m[15]. He put Terry Green (no relation) in as chief executive.

---

[15] The Telegraph

BHS and Iceland had a link that went back to 2000, when Malcolm Walker had made an agreement with BHS' previous owner Storehouse for a trial where Iceland products would be sold in the department store chain.[16] The prototype store-within-a store concept in Birmingham seemed to do quite well, so the two firms agreed to extend the trial to a further eight BHS stores.

While I was trying to get to grips with the numerous problems at Iceland, I took a quick look at the terms of the agreement between the two chains. The deal ran until December 2006 and gave Iceland an option to open up to 90 food stores in BHS shops by the end of 2001. The break clause in the contract said that whoever terminated the deal was liable to pay back any capital investment to the other party.

I was not particularly keen on the whole Iceland BHS arrangement, but I certainly wasn't about to saddle Iceland with an estimated £1.6 million liability by breaking off the deal. So, I decided to let it be and wait for them to come to me.

Sure enough, not long after I joined Iceland, Terry Green, the managing director of BHS, sidled up to me at a retail industry event and came right out with it.

"What about these Iceland stores in BHS?" was his opening gambit.

"Listen Terry, as you can no doubt see, I have some pretty big things to worry about right now," I said, referring to Iceland's much publicised troubles. "I couldn't really care less about nine of my stores inside your stores. They are way down my list of priorities."

We both left it at that for the moment. However, a few days later, Terry was on the phone to my office in Deeside, Wales.

"Shall we have a meeting about these stores?" he said.

Good, I thought. If you want Iceland out, then you are going to have to pay to get us out. An arrangement was made for me to go

---

[16] The Grocer

along to BHS' headquarters on the Marylebone Road in London. I decided to take two colleagues with me, my strategic director Norman Bell and Ellis O'Connor, a consultant who was shadowing me for a week. I agreed to let her do it as a favour because I had known her for a while and she was setting up a new company. Ellis wanted to get a feeling for the problems facing a chief executive.

On the day of the appointment, we were quickly taken up in the lift for the meeting at BHS. However, as we stepped out into the corridor, who should we see coming towards us with a broad smile and an outstretched hand but Philip Green himself. I quickly realised that Terry was not going to be involved in this at all. I would be in the hands of the famed retail tycoon.

Green led us into his large corner office, which was festooned with heavy wooden furniture and works of art propped up in every nook and cranny. It looked very different from the rest of the rather plain and anonymous-looking rooms we had passed on our way there.

Settling down into a large leather chair, I thought I had better start the meeting by blowing some smoke up Green's backside. He seemed to me like a man who would respond well to flattery.

"You've been doing pretty well, haven't you," I said. "You're taking over the High Street. Are you going to go into food next?"

Green seemed to respond quite well and launched into a dialogue about why he thought it wasn't worth buying a grocery chain because the margins were too thin and so on. Eventually though, the small talk dried up and I could tell the moment had come to talk business.

Green edged forward in his chair and looked straight into my eyes.

"Do you see all this around you?" he said, gesturing with his large arm around his office. "This is all mine. Every bit if it. I paid for it all out of my money.

"Everything I do in business is done with my money. You, on the other hand, are the chief executive of a public company. It is not your money that you are working with.

"So, why don't you take the decision to exit our stores? You can find a provision somewhere on your balance sheet to write the money off because it is not your money. Whereas, if I do it, then it comes out of my back pocket."

For a fraction of a second I was a little taken aback. I knew that Green had a bit of a reputation for being forthright and outspoken, but I had not expected this.

"Unfortunately Philip, I don't have a provision on my balance sheet for this issue," I began, collecting my thoughts as I went along. "For me to move a provision into something that doesn't pertain to it, is against account rules."

"More importantly than that, you need to know that as a chief executive, I treat my shareholders' money as if it were my money, so I couldn't do anything like that."

For a moment there was a complete silence.

"Alright, how much do you want to go?" said Green abruptly.

Perhaps it was the shock at how blatantly Green had been trying it on, or my surprise at the sudden volte-face. Or perhaps I figured he would negotiate, so I had better start high even though I knew the contract was only worth £1.6 million. Either way, what happened next was undoubtedly my biggest mistake in my relationship with the retail tycoon.

"Four million," I shot back bold as brass.

Looking back now, I still can't believe I said it. But, nothing could have prepared me for Green's response. Before the 'n' of the million has even died on my lips, he had launched himself out of his chair. His face was bright red and I swear his eyes looked like they might pop out of his head. It really did seem like smoke was actually billowing out of his ears and nostrils. And the torrent of abuse that was coming out of his mouth, well you would never have believed it if you had not heard it. He used every swear word I had ever heard and some new ones besides. They were delivered in such a breathless diatribe that they all seemed to gel together into one long, drawn-out, obscene expletive that seemed like it would never end.

The general gist of it was pretty clear though: why the fucking hell would he want to give me more than a couple of million, i.e. the correct amount?

After a minute of listening to this uninterrupted barrage, I couldn't stand it any more. I was so enraged by this outrageous behaviour and the torrent of words that were vibrating through my brain that I too leapt to my feet. I could feel my blood boiling and my heart racing thanks to the adrenalin pumping through my body. I had never, in my whole life, been spoken to like this. I was not about to lie down and take it now. It was vile. For a few seconds the red mist descended and I only had one thought on my mind; I had to hit him. Hard. I had to make him stop the tirade.

Then, somehow, I composed myself. I would be as bad as him if I tried to flatten him. I would be letting myself, my family and my colleagues down.

"Stop right now," I said, raising my hand as though fending off a charging bull. "You stop. No one in the world gets to speak to me like that.

"I don't have to stay in a place where I get spoken to like this, so I am going to leave. Just make out a cheque for whatever is on the contract because we are finished."

I turned around and for the first time since the altercation began, I saw the open-mouthed expressions on the faces on my two colleagues. They were clearly struggling to process what they had just witnessed. Motioning for them to follow, I made for the door.

Amazingly, although Green had stopped shouting, it was not all over. As we crossed the room, Green took a step forward and grabbed the arm of Norman Bell pulling him back into the room.

Giving my colleague a warm look as though he was his best friend ever, Green said: "When you get back to the office, give me a ring and we will do a deal."

I could hardly believe it. After all that had just transpired, he was carrying on like nothing had happened and still trying to negotiate.

"You didn't understand me, did you?" I said, raising my voice in my exasperation. "Look in my eyes and listen to what I say, very, very, clearly. You and I are finished and I will never speak to you again and that is the end of that."

I had made a huge mistake in my negotiation with Green, but his reaction was completely unacceptable. (As an aside, I have since heard that when he told the story to other people in the industry, it was him that slung me out of his office, rather than me walking out.)

Looking back on this, in the cold light of day, I can now make a number of observations.

Although I don't agree with his rambunctious style of management, it cannot be denied that Sir Philip, as he now is, has been immensely successful with his retail empire. The tycoon clearly knows what works on the High Street and is dogged in his pursuit of success and expansion.

However, this incident with Sir Philip, although extreme, epitomises a lot of the leadership you find in the retail business. Yes, there are a lot of entertaining, larger-than-life, characters in this sector, which makes the High Street an interesting place to work, but there is a lot of bullying and posturing at the top too. If you are lower down the ranks and unable to defend yourself, it can sometimes make it an uncomfortable, difficult place to be.

The difference between Sir Philip and many of the other heads of retail businesses is: there are plenty others who utterly fail to see the bigger picture. The man (or woman) at the top is so consumed by playing the boss and making sure that everyone knows it, that they end up destroying the chains they run. They completely take their eye off the ball.

My view is that the poor and sometimes eccentric leadership that characterises some of our best known High Street names has played its own part in the gradual erosion of some of the chains in this sector. This is why we need to look at the problem that comes from within.

I am unlucky enough to have first hand knowledge of just how bad problems with leadership can get, because I was on the sidelines of one of the biggest fraud cases in retail history. Although the characters at the head of Wickes, the company embroiled in the fraud, were subsequently cleared after a lengthy court case, no one should lose sight of the fact that something very bad happened at the firm. For some reason, certain people in this organisation felt compelled to go outside the normal practices of business and make claims that simply were not true.

The events that occurred in the nineties at DIY retailer Wickes brought the company to its knees and put thousands of jobs under threat. Many hundreds of people were made redundant in the aftermath of the scandal and millions of pounds were wiped off the company's share price.

Let me share the facts as I know them.

I was working for Wickes in South Africa before the crisis struck. Then, as far as I and everyone else was concerned, the DIY group was riding high. I was looking forward to returning to the UK shortly to take up a new appointment running the firm's stores on home soil. In the four years leading up to 1996, profits had been rising steadily and the chain was the toast of the sector. It was an exciting prospect.

Overnight though, everything changed.

In June 1996, after the discovery of a file from the Dutch side of the business, Wickes admitted that its profits had been overstated by some £53 million over the previous four years. Its market capitalisation went from £500 million to zero overnight and its shares were briefly suspended.

I had arrived in the UK in early June, but now the company was in tatters and teetering on the edge of bankruptcy. Practically all of the top executives had been sacked or suspended and I was the last senior man standing. The banks and non executive directors, who were now in control, appointed me chief executive of this basket case. This meant that in the ensuing five years I was given a ringside seat to observe the investigation into how corporate disasters happen.

PricewaterhouseCoopers, who replaced the original auditors Arthur Anderson, were installed into the office next to mine and ended up being there for a long time. They went through everything in minute detail. The Serious Fraud Office (SFO) was also involved and they quickly released a statement saying that in the period of January 1994 to June 1996, Wickes overstated its financial position thanks to 'inappropriate recognition of supplier rebate and contribution income'.

Five former Wickes directors were charged in connection with the accounting scandal: Henry Sweetbaum, the chairman and chief executive; Trefor Llewellyn, the group finance director; Geoffrey Battersby, the group financial controller; Terrence Carson, the finance director of Wickes' main retailing operating subsidiary; and Leslie Rosenthal, the group trading director responsible for buying.

The allegation was that the company had devised a 'two letter' system, which enabled Wickes' buyers to book substantial payments from suppliers to inflate profits in a single year.

How did this work? Well rebates, also known as Long Term Agreements (LTAs), are a common thing in the retail trade and there is nothing particularly wrong with that, although it is a clumsy system and occasionally open to abuse. What happens is, a supplier will agree to give a store group buyer a discount at the end of the year if a predetermined buying target is reached. So, say the shop bought 100 of the supplier's widgets, as agreed, then at the end of the agreed period, the supplier would give them a one per cent rebate.

The rebates themselves are generally quite low, just one or two per cent in the grocery business, but for reasons lost in the mists of time they were a little higher, around seven per cent, in the DIY and building products world.

What appeared to happen at Wickes was that the level of these rebates was systematically overstated. The usual seven per cent rose to eight per cent, then nine per cent the following year and ten the year after that. No one, not even the auditors, questioned these double digit LTAs.

Some effort was clearly made by the person behind this to cover their tracks. Hence the 'two letter' system. Suppliers were writing two letters, essentially referring to the LTA, but both saying quite different things. One letter would signal an agreement by the supplier to pay rebates of X, provided the shop group bought a predetermined amount. It would refer to two or even three years of volume to be bought by the retailer. Another letter would allude to the same percentage rebate, but this time would call the sum a contribution to the retailer for 'marketing' their products that year.

Agreeing to a rebate is perfectly legal and above board, but, if you agree to one on the strength of an agreement for two, three or even more years of volume, then the benefit of that rebate has to be disbursed across the following two, three, or more years' accounts. The accountants didn't do that though, because all they saw was a letter saying that a benefit of X per cent was coming in for 'marketing' in that year.

As the scale of the fraud grew, so did the inventiveness. Wickes held piles of letters from eager suppliers apparently offering hundreds of thousands in rebates each year. What these letters did not show was that someone had clearly given those same suppliers the green light to raise their prices the following year, to claw back those hundreds of thousands of pounds. The rebates were being paid for out of the cost price the following year. Eventually, and inevitably, the cash flow went out of kilter with the profit declaration. The whole thing had to go pop.

It took the SFO many years to unravel this and it culminated in a highly complex ten-month trial at Southwark Crown Court. This trial involved more than one million documents and witnesses coming from as far afield as South Korea and China. It was estimated that the whole thing cost in excess of £40 million to investigate and prosecute[17]. However, in September 2002, Battersby was cleared and two months later Sweetbaum, Llewellyn and Carson were acquitted too. In June the following year, Rosenthal walked free after a separate trial.

The SFO was inevitably castigated for wasting public money on failed prosecutions and the episode revived the debate about the wisdom of using the jury trial system to prosecute complex corporate cases. However, to me, the entire episode raised far wider issues. I spent five years at Wickes in the aftermath of that corporate disaster, doing my best to turn the company around before finally selling it to Focus for £325 million[18]. It was a long, tough and often extremely frustrating job.

The big issue for me is (and always has been) that someone put the company in a position where this turnaround was necessary.

Whether or not it was one person, or a handful of them, things were done that placed the company in a downward spiral from which it was extremely lucky to recover from. Looking at it in the context of a problem that begins from within, one cannot help but conclude that there was some sort of a failure of leadership at Wickes in the early nineties. You have to ask the question: could it have been the case that people within Wickes felt under such extreme pressure because they were obliged to produce ever more spectacular results year by year? Were they put under so much stress that they were prepared to break the law?

Looking back now at my early days in Wickes, I can confirm it was once an extraordinarily pressurised environment. Henry Sweetbaum, the American businessman who was its long-term chief executive, was a forthright leader who did not suffer fools gladly. Sweetbaum's leadership

---

[17] http://www.telegraph.co.uk/finance/2834729/Ex-Wickes-trio-cleared-of-fraud.html
[18] www.dukestreet.com

style had certainly got results in the past too. He rescued Wickes in 1980, when it was part of the ailing US Wickes Companies Group, and went on to make it one of the UK's biggest DIY companies. He led its float on the London Stock Market in 1986 after turnover had almost doubled over the preceding three years.

Every year, Wickes would hold a spectacular event at the Runnymede-on-Thames Hotel in Egham, Surrey. Buyers and key suppliers would be wined and dined in luxury surroundings while they discussed what offers, discounts and rebates would be on offer for the following year. It was made very clear to all parties that anything that smacked of same-as-last-year was not going to cut it. The pressure was relentless.

Is this how accounting scandals begin? On the evidence, it certainly seems like it played its part. This is not to suggest that Sweetbaum had any knowledge of the double letters, or any other aspect of the fraud. Indeed, it has been publically stated by a court of law that he did not. However, what cannot be denied is he presided over a regime where this type of activity grew at an alarming rate.

Sweetbaum and the senior team created an environment where leadership-by-fear prospered. That can, and generally does, produce impressive results in the short-term, but in the long-term it can prove to be highly destructive. Leadership-by-fear is simply not sustainable nor should it be acceptable.

Many leaders, and not just in the retail sector either, find it hugely gratifying to be told their team fears them. In an environment like this, things can be demanded and done, questions are never asked and the man or woman at the top is never challenged. Everything moves forward smoothly. Or does it?

In a fear-based regime, no one will ever feel emboldened to come forward with ideas of how to do things better. They will never be fully committed to the business, or hugely supportive of any new initiatives. It is quite likely they will do what is expected of them and no more and also employee turnover, absenteeism and lateness will be extraordinarily high.

In the long run, this absence of motivation, vision, creativity, loyalty and planning can and will take its toll.

Like I said, this is not a syndrome solely attributable to retail, but I have to say it has been extraordinarily widespread in this industry. Bosses in the shop business have long seemed determined to stamp their mark and emphasise their dominance. It has been a problem that has characterised the industry right up until the turn of the millennium and there are still pockets of it today.

I myself became aware of it early on in my career while at Bishops Food Stores. The four directors of this chain of stores were all descended from the family founders and had clearly had an immensely privileged upbringing. The retailer was a PLC by the time I became a buyer there in my early twenties, but the founding family still called the shots. And, as if to mark their superiority, they all insisted on being called by the prefix 'Mister' followed by their first name. Thus, Roger and Nigel Harvey were known as Mr Roger and Mr Nigel, while John and Michael Bradfield were addressed as Mr John and Mr Michael.

To emphasise their superiority, the four directors and other senior executives had their own dining room at company HQ and their own executive loo. Everything about them signalled that they had complete control over all decisions within the company. Indeed, they rarely trusted subordinates with anything which might have any far-reaching impact.

This hierarchical approach to business creates barriers at every level. Communication grinds to a halt and that in itself is quite harmful. If you add in a leader who couples this division with arrogant, autocratic, or even dictatorial, behaviour then you will create the worst possible environment. It will manifest itself in confused and poor performance among the team below because there is no clear direction. Employees will feel unable to say what they think because their views count for so little that they are not even allowed into certain parts of the building.

Bishops is not the only retailer to have adopted such a culture. Stories abound in the retail industry of such nuances. Clothing retailer C&A, for example, also clung on to the 'Mister' prefix, right up until the time when they were forced to pull out of the UK in June 2000, shutting 109 stores after clocking up £250 million of losses over the previous five years. That was not the only eccentricity at the department store either. The family motto of the Dutch brothers who founded the clothing store chain was: Openness is a Sign of Weakness. Clemens and August Brenninkmeijer – their C&A initials are the basis for the store's name – also stamped their authority by declaring that sales figures should never, ever, be uttered out loud. Right up until 1997, managers had to use a complex code to report the day's takings to the head office. The code was based on the name of Joseph Alberdingk, a respected poet and philosopher, with each letter of the surname representing a number from zero to nine. Staff would translate each number into the corresponding letter and then extend the letter into a Christian name.

Thus, a manager may be in the ludicrous situation of reporting over the telephone to head office that the day's takings were: Betty, Lucy, Albert and four Ks.

In true le Carré style, and just to make sure that everyone understood their place in the hierarchy, staff had to take oaths of secrecy about the code. They were also only initiated into it after an intense period of training and then only once they had achieved executive status.

Another retailer famed for its deeply hierarchical approach is British High Street darling Marks & Spencer. The supremacy of the chairman as an all-powerful being, with almost divine powers of governance, continued right up and into the nineties. Questioning the chairman, or vigorous debate of the issues, simply was not done. Flagrant disagreement was viewed as a resigning matter, but most of the time, people were too scared to say what they thought anyhow.

Sir Richard Greenbury, the chairman and chief executive of M&S between 1988 to 1999, was a notoriously intimidating presence in and out of the boardroom. During his tenure, the company smashed the £1 billion profit barrier and one of his most popular reposts to anyone who had the temerity to question him on anything was; "If we are getting it so wrong, why are we making more than £1 billion a year?"[19]

Of course, as we all now know, something was indeed going very wrong at M&S and not long after they had reached that £1 billion figure, profits at the clothing and food giant slumped by a shocking 23 per cent in the first half of 1998[20]. The chain has struggled to retain its former glory ever since.

The other problem with the autocratic style found at Bishops, Wickes, M&S, C&A and in numerous other retailers besides, is the attitude always spreads through the whole organisation. Yes, everyone is terrified of the person at the top and hates the culture of fear, but they all become accustomed to operating in this way. Management by fear – and all of the problems that that brings with it – cascades down the company with each level bullying the next in line. The abused becomes the abuser. Having become used to operating in a particular way, with little thought to emotion or empathy, people further down the organisation adopt this stance in dealing with others. And who can blame them? It is all they know.

The result? Everyone becomes obsessed about jockeying for rank and prestige in order to protect their position, whether or not it is at the expense of doing their job properly. This was true to such a degree in M&S, for example, that executives became fixated on badges of their seniority. The fact that the company encouraged this by quirky symbols of this, did nothing to help. Senior staff would eye each other jealously to see how many big square windows the offices of their colleague sported, the depth of pile of their office carpet (yes, the higher up in rank you were, the thicker your carpet) and what car they drove.

To me this is all nonsense and has no place in a modern, well run, retailer. Yes, there are times when a private, executive, dining room may be handy because senior executives may need to have a quiet, confidential chat with a fellow director, but none of this is ever really necessary. You

[19] The Rise and Fall of Marks & Spencer, Judi Bevan, Profile Books, 2001
[20] http://news.bbc.co.uk/1/hi/business/206742.stm

could just as easily get a plate of sandwiches put into the boardroom. There is no need for a statement saying; you are different. Retail leaders should be trying to break down barriers, not shore them up.

All this scrabbling for status does is to totally sap the energy from the business and block any vigour and drive from the ranks down below. The knock-on effect is a bland and unadventurous style of doing business. No one lower down the organisation will be willing to stick their neck out and be creative because they are scared of making a mistake and being singled out. Worse still is the response where subordinates desperately try to impress their bosses and keep out of harm's way by constantly pulling rabbits out of the hat in whatever way they can, just as apparently happened at Wickes.

This sense that 'anything goes as long as the job is done' creates a very anarchic, unregulated firm, which can be extremely damaging in the long-term. One of the best examples of this I became aware of was at Tesco in the late seventies. Back then, a practice known as 'bung and shuffle' was rife.

Bung and Shuffle worked a bit like this: Suppliers would visit Tesco's sprawling headquarters in Cheshunt, Hertfordshire and pitch their wares to buyers. They'd tell them about their lavish marketing campaign, show off their great point of sale packaging and then make a fantastic discount offer on the understanding the grocery giant agreed to a certain sized of order. If they were lucky and had a good product, they may get a deal. So far, so good. All systems go.

Except it wasn't.

In those days, Tesco had divided its store empire up and down the UK into segments called regional managing directorships (RMDs). At the head of each RMD was a person who was more powerful than any buyer in Cheshunt. In fact, each RMD was run like a mini fiefdom.

Once a supplier had done a deal with head office, they would have to visit each RMD in turn in order to secure distribution in their geographical group of stores. Inclusion was by no means guaranteed, but to stand any chance of getting the products listed, a 'gift' such as a Rolex watch would usually be required to smooth the deal.

Although it was known by the rather quaint term of 'bung and shuffle', this colloquialism hid the fact that the practice was actually very damaging on a number of levels. Tesco was not acting like the cohesive, well run, company it is today. People were not engaged and moving in the right direction. The culture was all wrong and the buying practices were not to anyone's advantage.

When I was recruited to Tesco in the mid eighties, Ian MacLaurin had already stamped out bung and shuffle, but this still hadn't ironed out all the inherent problems, in fact, I coined a phrase for the senior executives there like these RMDs who ruled by fear: leather jacketed bully boys. Back then, they were evident at all levels, not just the RMDs, but in the boardroom too. I was fortunate that (a) this organisation was prepared to hear me out on this one, and (b) they could see that they had to change if they wanted to move the company forward.

By way of some background, I joined Tesco when I was 34 years old and the job title they gave me was customer services director. There had not been a customer services director before and I have to confess, I thought it might be a bit of a poisoned chalice.

John Gildersleeve, who was then the personnel and marketing director, explained to me the thinking behind the appointment. Ian MacLaurin, who had recently been made chairman at Tesco, was concerned about the grocery chain's reputation. Tesco had built hundreds of stores across the UK, including dozens of out-of-town superstores, yet the public still thought of them rather derisively as a pile it high, sell it cheap destination. MacLaurin wanted to change the way the British public felt about Tesco.

My initial thoughts were; I don't know the first thing about this, or how to go about it. Up until that time, my expertise was in fresh foods. I loved produce and doing displays. What did I know about transforming customer perception?

Never one to turn down a challenge, I asked for three months' grace, plus a nominal budget, in order to do some research. Then I got stuck in. I did internal surveys, brought in consultants and read lots of books on business theory. Nothing was taboo, even though asking lots of questions internally was not the 'Tesco way' back then. I was given a job to do, so I did it.

After three exhausting months, I was ready.

I prepared a presentation which was to be made to Dennis Tuffin, the retail operations director. It took place at Tuffin's cramped office in Maidstone on Christmas Eve. I can still remember now my feeling of nervousness as I began my presentation. I knew what I was about to say would ruffle a fair few feathers. I might even get kicked out on my arse.

"I can't do this job because the issue is not with the organisation," I began. Then, taking a deep breath I continued to the nub of the matter. "The problem lies with you, the guys on the board.

"You are all a bunch of leather jacketed bully boys who pride yourselves on the fact you eat babies for breakfast. That is why you have got a problem.

"There is nothing about the management style or approach in Tesco which gives the team lower down a sense of belonging. Why should a checkout girl smile and greet customers when she is paid peanuts? What is more, she knows that when one of you guys walk into her store you won't even stop to talk to them, unless it is to tell them off.

"This bullying attitude has got to stop and it has to stop from the top. If you want to start viewing customers as the most important thing to this organisation – and we do have to do that – the most effective way to do this is through the people who serve them. The only way to do that is to have a management style that is engaging and gives people a sense of belonging. It all starts with you."

For a moment Dennis didn't say a word and I started to wonder if I had blown it. Then he picked up the phone to Gildersleeve.

"Bill is here and this guy has the answer," he barked, after the barest of pleasantries to Gildersleeve. "John, we have to put this presentation on the agenda for the first meeting after Christmas."

Tuffin then turned to me and told me to go away, polish up my presentation and be ready to present it to the board in the first week of January.

Come January, I did the presentation again, although this time it was in the spacious and slightly intimidating surroundings of Tesco's boardroom in Cheshunt, Hertfordshire. By this time, I had renamed my findings, 'Customer is King'.

I was incredibly nervous about what the reaction might be – after all I was accusing this massive organisation of being led by leather jacketed bully boys. This might not be what they wanted to hear.

Once again, there was a complete silence when I had finished. Then, the chairman Ian MacLaurin spoke.

"Well, I don't think we need to debate this, do we?" he began.

As he was saying this, I was practically screaming inside my head; yes, we do need to debate it! That is what this is all about. This is what I have been saying for the last 30 minutes. *You are supposed to get consensus.*

But MacLaurin had not finished.

"This sort of thinking is long overdue in this boardroom," he went on. "We should all get behind what Bill has just proposed and back him hook, line and sinker. Am I clear?"

I never did get the chance to talk to the chairman about the irony of his approach in the light of what I had just been saying, but the good thing is everyone did get Full Square behind this more approachable, collegiate, stance.

The Customer is King strategy was adapted into Tesco Customer First and in a very short space of time, took on a life of its own. Senior executives completely changed their approach and you could really see the change on the ground floor. Instead of ignoring colleagues until they told them off for some misdemeanour, or walking around the stores with their hands behind their backs growling at people, executives started having eye contact with the team in stores. They talked to them about issues that they might have.

The chain started to have a much better feel to it and it really did translate into the way the team interacted with customers.

This is not to say that all the executives found the transition easy. One Friday evening, for example, I got a call from Dennis Tuffin who immediately got to the point.

"That you, Grimsey?" he yelled into the phone.

"Yes, Dennis," I replied. "What's up?"

"Pin your ears back, I need to give you a bollocking," he bawled.

"What have I done?" I asked, wracking my brains as to what it might be.

"You haven't done anything, but I am just fed up with being so effing nice to everybody all week that I have to give someone a bollocking!"

Poor Dennis. He had had to change his whole approach to dealing with people. But, to give him credit, he did and he did it well.

In many ways Tesco was, as usual, ahead of its time in understanding the need to transform its approach to customer services and to make that change from the very top. MacLaurin and his team identified the problem, seized the moment and did something to change it.

The lesson I learned here, and in my other experiences in the sector, is retail needs strong, focused, leadership. The rigid, unyielding, management by fear techniques which can still be found in some chains today belong to the last century.

Retailing is, I would contend, very unlike any other business sector. It is a highly competitive, fast paced, industry, which is almost instantly susceptible to economic swings. Most importantly, it is a people business.

The ever-changing whims of the customer can make or break a store chain because the barrow that you wheel out into the market may be all the rage today, but it might well be a one-hit wonder and rejected tomorrow. Creating a sustainable retail business is not a matter of luck. You have to communicate with your team and your customers and listen carefully to what they have to say.

Of course, if a chain reaches any scale at all, the person at the top has to deal with communicating and motivating staff at multiple sites because it is them that are on the front line. In Tesco's case, that means 492,714 staff in 5,380 stores worldwide[21]. Just saying that you want to be 'more customer focused' doesn't mean it will happen without a lot of thought and a herculean effort.

None of this is to say that our High Street chains have not moved on. Many have. Indeed, in the past 20 years there have been some extraordinary developments in retail, many of which have been emulated elsewhere in other industries. One of the best documented is the transformation of supermarket chain Asda by Archie Norman and Allan Leighton. When the pair arrived at Asda in the early nineties, the chain was, in their words, a 'basket case' after a series of dreadful management decisions. True to form, they discovered an area in Asda's Leeds HQ which was called the 'directorate', which was solely for executives where the quality of the offices and furnishings indicated that person's position in the hierarchy. Leighton, who had initially been allocated an office in the directorate, picked up his things and went to sit with his team in the marketing department. Before long, he and Norman physically and symbolically removed all the walls and divisions in Asda House and a new culture was born.

The pair wore badges bearing their Christian names, just like everyone else did. It broke down barriers and encouraged people around the firm to speak to them. People were called 'colleagues', not staff, adding to their sense of worth in the firm and Norman and Leighton made sure they were always highly visible in stores. They were ready to listen. Ideas were rewarded and not ridiculed.

---

[21] www.tescoplc.com

This and a wealth of other approachable strategies worked too. In a matter of years, the company was transformed from that basket case worth £500 million, into one sold to US giant Walmart for £6.2 billion in 1999.

Not all of their ideas were new. Leighton readily admits that he borrowed shamelessly from the innovative ideas of Julian Richer, the founder of hi-fi empire Richer Sounds. Richer's philosophy is that all his colleagues share in the success of his company and are rewarded for their hard work. Thus, each month, the people who work at the best performing branch of Richer Sounds are lent a Rolls Royce. Richer also funds 15 holiday homes all over Europe for his team and gives everyone a day off on their birthdays. It is all designed to make everyone feel valued and part of a team. The knock-on effect is it is reflected in everything the team does, there is a buzz about the place and customers do notice the difference.

I am not adverse to copying good ideas either and confess that I used many of these techniques when I was chief executive of various chains. I had the name Bill sewn into all my work shirts and wore the same type of shirt as all my colleagues in stores. This signalled to everyone that, just because I was captain, didn't mean I was any different as a person. I only had to behave differently as a leader.

At Wickes, for example, I began a 'Big Breakfast' where each month I would go to a store somewhere in the UK and invite a range of colleagues from that store to eat with me. It might be a forklift truck operator, a checkout operator and a store manager. I'd say to them; there are only three objectives to this event. The first was to have a damn good nosh-up, because they didn't often get the chance in the working day. The second was for me to tell them more about the company. The third, and most important, was for me to hear about what was happening in Wickes, stuff that I never got to hear about in the ivory towers of head office.

I'd get to hear that Product X was never available. Or that they had had to put a work-around into the new computer system that had cost millions of pounds to install because otherwise they could not do something as basic as offer refunds. Those breakfasts were a real eye-opener.

One of the most effective strategies by far was to spend time actually working in store. I would spend a whole week there, working in various positions, including a long spell on the checkouts. It was amazing what I would find out.

At Wickes, for example, I made an interesting discovery about how our stock control systems were going awry. Back then, we had 4,000 Stock Keeping Units (SKU), or different product lines, and head office worked very hard to ensure that our best selling lines did not go out of stock. If any one store had more than 20 out-of-stocks in one day, then questions would be asked and investigations launched.

When I was working in one store, I discovered boxes and boxes of single samples of key products. What had happened is, the canny managers had worked out that if they slipped one of each of the slower selling lines into a box and stored it in the back, they would never be out-of-stock. The computer would show, quite rightly, that there was still one left. Yes, they were manipulating the results, but at least they didn't have anyone coming round to investigate. This was a throw-back to the fear-management days, the problem was; that wasn't good for the business.

The only way to find out things like this is to go out and work in the store. The Mr Johns or Mr Rogers of this world would never do that and, in the long run, that is to the detriment of their businesses.

The essence of good retail leadership is to engage with individuals on your team. Indeed, look at it in another way; shop work can be the most boring occupation in the world if you feel put upon and unappreciated. Sitting at a till all day listening to the scanner go beep, beep, beep and knowing you are earning the minimum wage for the pleasure is not exactly a motivating prospect. The onus is therefore upon retail leaders to show that people have an important role in an organisation. This in turn will help colleagues to serve customers well and enhance their experience.

It is a massive challenge. Even though much of the retail sector has moved on a long way from the days of code words, Mr prefixes and bung and shuffle, there are still remnants of these practices in evidence.

It does the industry no favours and does not equip it to deal with the trials ahead.

Once again, the industry cannot move forward while it continues to repeat the mistakes of the past. There is no going back. If it wants to move on though, it has to be forward thinking.

Chapter Three
Finance – Retail's house of cards

The scale and recklessness of dealmaking on the High Street in the boom years played a significant role in the erosion and even collapse of many of our household names.

I t's Saturday 18 December 2004 and, with the economy booming, High Streets up and down the land have been flooded with Christmas shoppers. Goods are flying off the shelves and the general mood is overwhelmingly positive.

Except for where I am.

I've been holed up in UBS Warburg's offices in London's Finsbury Avenue for what seems like a lifetime. Surrounded by lawyers, advisors and financial experts, we are deep in discussions over the sale of The Big Food Group PLC. I've been chief executive at the company since January 2001 and it's not been an easy ride. Shortly after I arrived it emerged that expected profits of circa £140m were more likely to be closer to £40m and in an emergency board meeting at our London lawyers we lost both the chairman, Malcolm Walker and the finance director in a scene which would not have looked out of place on a Hollywood film. Then, after issuing several profits warnings within weeks of arriving, I had a constant battle to keep the company on its feet.

The reason? The Big Food Group was saddled with £600 million of debt following its purchase of the food wholesaler Booker for £373.5 million in the year 2000 and it had been like dragging a permanent dead weight behind us.

A lot of people had scratched their heads at the time of the deal, wondering what Iceland, a frozen food retailer, was doing buying a food wholesale company like Booker, particularly when the price tag was so crippling. The Big Food Group did have a small wholesale operation, Woodward, but even so, it felt like a deal too far.

Delving into it more deeply though, it was clear Malcolm Walker, the then-head of The Big Food Group, had his reasons. Iceland, the company at the heart of The Big Food Group which he founded in 1970 in Owestry, Shropshire with a £30 investment[22], had lost its way a little in the late nineties. Having initially soared on the back of the then popular 'buy one, get one free' phenomenon, sales suddenly slumped. Iceland had caught the 'green' bug, and after initially banning artificial colours and flavours from all the chain's own brand foods, they went one step further and sensationally contracted to buy over 30 per cent of the *world's* then organic vegetable crop in a three-year deal.

Sadly, the average hard-stretched, customer did not share Iceland's enthusiasm for organic foods and the sight of oddly shaped, mismatched, natural fruit and veg did not capture their imagination. In fact, as was recorded at the time, sales fell off a cliff.

Lack of enthusiasm for organics among their customer base wasn't their only problem either. They were acutely aware that their chain, like so many British businesses at the time, was facing a massive pension deficit. Casting around for ideas on how to boost the business, their gaze fell upon Booker which was operating well and also had a pension scheme in significant surplus.

Iceland wooed its shareholders to support the proposal to buy Booker by assuring them that Iceland was the UK's fastest growing supermarket, with like-for-like sales at a mouth-watering six per cent. What they omitted to say was that this six per cent was actually based on till rings, not actual sales. Every time a customer took advantage of Iceland's ubiquitous 'buy one, get one free' deals, two products were rung through the till even though cold, hard, cash was only being paid for the one product. If any investors cared to challenge the information more deeply, they would have established that Iceland's cash sale like-for-likes were actually closer to just one per cent, which put Iceland at the bottom end of the supermarket like-for-like league tables.

But, as is often the case in these too-good-to-be-true deals, no one looked too deeply and boom, the two companies were put together in an apparently fantastic deal.

---

[22] www.iceland.co.uk

Of course, as I discovered when I joined The Big Food Group seven months after the deal was done, it was not so fantastic after all. For a kick-off, it was immediately obvious that, by then, sales had actually slid into negative territory and little had been done to realise the £30 million of cost synergies promised in the prospectus. Instead of the projected profit of £140 million, the underlying profit of the business was more like £40 million. The business was not going nearly as well as investors thought and there was very little I could do about it because the group was already saddled with £600 million of debt.

Not surprisingly, when all of this come to light, the investors were none too pleased.

I had very few options but to refinance the debt and that meant convincing the banks, who were in control of the company, that I had a plan to turn this company around. Somehow, we managed to convince them and set about raising £300 million of new debt from the banks, which reduced the original sum to £300 million. We also raised a further £150 million from a high yield bond and sold the freeholds of Iceland and Booker properties to raise the rest of the cash we needed just to stay afloat. It wasn't the perfect solution. The yields we got on the new deals were awful – we were effectively paying 9.5 per cent interest on the new debt – plus the property deal saddled the company with crippling rents to lease its own stores.

The following few years were just one financial juggling act after another. In fact, in the whole time I was at The Big Food Group, I must have spent 99 per cent of my time sorting out the problems caused by this massive debt. I barely had a moment to do anything to do with retailing or trading. I didn't have the time to use the benefit of my experience and knowledge to move the company on, innovate and spot new opportunities. I had become a financier.

To go back to the analogy I have used time and again about wheeling out my barrow into the market place, at The Big Food Group, I was forced into a situation where I had to rely on the fact that others were setting out my stall for me. The fact that my barrow was put out in the morning and taken in at night was the best I could really hope for when my mind was clearly distracted elsewhere. As you can imagine, this is hardly the scenario that gets a retailer noticed. It doesn't move a shop forward. It certainly doesn't benefit shareholders and, more than likely, there will be some keen young fellow around who will notice your barrow looking a bit old, stale, and uncared for and who will go all out to make his or her market stall the best, most exciting place to be in the whole market.

That is how retailers lose their way, get overtaken and even collapse altogether. In my own case, my absolute absorption with debt meant I did miss things. Having issued several profit warnings over what had gone on before I arrived, I had the ignominy of putting one out that happened on my watch too. I had been so busy dealing with the debt problems that I managed to miss the fact that we had lost control of the margin at Iceland. Despite continuing and even upping the practice of 'buy one, get one free', or even 'buy three, get two free', we were slow to pick up on the fact that sales were not going up. None of our promotions were dropping through to the bottom line. I had no alternative but to issue yet another profit warning in the summer of 2002.

Eventually, four years in at The Big Food Group, I felt my back was against the wall. I had done everything to take advantage of the synergies at the group, including move HR, finance and IT into head office and closing down satellite offices elsewhere, but it made very little difference to the bottom line as sales were not keeping pace with cost inflation. It was obvious to me that the glaring reality of the situation was that an integrated food group like The Big Food Group just wasn't going to work. It was the wrong strategy and, even if it were the right one, it would take a hell of a lot of money to make a success of it. That was, of course, money we didn't have and never had had.

In my view, the only way the component parts could survive and move on was if The Big Food Group was broken up. However, breaking up a PLC is never an easy thing to do. The sum of the parts never quite adds up.

There was, however, a way out. At the same time as I was starting to think enough is enough, The Big Food Group came under the radar of the super-acquisitive investment vehicle Baugur. Since 2001, the Icelandic group had been leading a breathtaking raid on some of the UK High Street's best known names. The previously unknown group, led by charismatic young Icelanders Jon Asgeir Johannesson and Tryggvi Jonsson, had built up a 20 per cent stake in Topshop-to-Burton chain Arcadia, before being forced to withdraw from a full bid after being stymied by a (unconnected) fraud investigation. But, not to be stopped for long, Baugur had built up controlling stakes in fashion chains Oasis and Coast and had significant investments in department store House of Fraser, supermarket chain Somerfield and sports chain JJB Sports. It had also bought outright the Hamleys toy store, jewellery chain Goldsmiths, and fashion chains Whistles, Karen Millen and MK One.

The Big Food Group was also clearly on its shopping list. Since October 2002, when it acquired 15 per cent of the chain's shares, it had continued to quietly build up its stake.

By late 2004, at about the same time I had fully resolved that the only option for The Big Food Group was to break it up, Baugur owned 22 per cent of the stock.[23]

I picked up the phone and called Jon Asgeir Johannesson.

"This business needs to be broken up," I said after the usual pleasantries. "I believe the only way to do this is to take it private and so it makes sense for you to buy it.

"Would you like to meet up?"

And that's how I came to be sitting in UBS Warburg's offices in late December 2004, locked in talks about selling the Iceland chain to a team from Iceland (a newspaper headline-writer's gift – as we were to later discover).

The negotiations went on long into the night and it was all pretty intense as these things always are. At around midnight, we finally came to an agreement for a £326 million cash takeover of The Big Food Group, netting shareholders a respectable 95 pence a share.[24]

[23] www.ft.com
[24] www.ft.com

Although I felt an overwhelming sense of relief that the deal had been done and that it was the best possible outcome, I still had one nagging doubt.

Turning to the Baugur advisors, who were busy packing away their files, I asked the question that had been troubling me for a while now: "Before we go public on this tomorrow morning, where is the money?"

I was not alone in questioning just how Baugur was financing its audacious raids on the British High Street. Although many struggling retail brands could not believe their luck when they were snapped up by the Icelandics, the source of their cash was shrouded in mystery. There were disparaging rumours that they were laundering money for the Russian mafia, but the truth when it emerged a few years later was far more extraordinary.

Baugur's whirlwind spree of acquisitions was funded through excessive borrowing and a complex web of ownership structures. Even the bankers who advised Johannesson on his spending spree later admitted the deals were fantastically complicated. Much of the funding was generated via Icelandic banks that offered eager investors such fantastic rates of interest that it eventually led to the collapse of the country's entire financial system.

However, British banks and, most significantly, HBOS, were providing some of Baugur's funding too and it was a British bank which was to finance The Big Food Group deal. Which brings me to Peter Cummings, the director of corporate lending at HBOS, who was at the forefront of billions of pounds of deals in the retail industry in the late nineties and early 2000s. Under his watch, HBOS expanded its debt operations tenfold. Cummings backed some of the biggest retail deals of the era, including loans to the Barclay brothers to buy Littlewoods (£840 million), £600 million for the sale and leaseback of the Woolworths' property portfolio by the Livingstone brothers and then the biggest cheque in HBOS's history when he provided Philip Green with £950 million to buy Arcadia in 2002.[25]

---

[25] http://www.dailymail.co.uk/news/article-1145647/A-660-000-pay-man-broke-HBOS.html

On that December night in 2004, I got to see first-hand, how powerful this man had become. Two hours after asking "show me the money", a letter arrived. It was from Cummings himself and it confirmed HBOS would be underwriting the entire £326 million deal to buy The Big Food Group.

I was dumbfounded. I had never seen anything like it.

"Is that it?" I asked the advisors, showing them the signed letter. "Is that enough? This means we can go public now?"

They nodded in assent and the deal went ahead. I still wake up even now and think: how did that happen? How did one man become so powerful that a single letter from him was enough to kick-start the sale of companies that were worth many millions?

Cummings' story makes fascinating reading. He joined the Bank of Scotland as a tea boy in 1973 and worked his way up through the ranks. By 2001, he was managing director of corporate banking at the bank and there are signs that by then his bosses had begun to give him a pretty much open chequebook. Bank of Scotland had merged with Halifax in that year and the combined entity was apparently desperate to expand its corporate loan book. Cummings had impressed the board with a few deals, particularly those with retail supremo Philip Green and although it was obvious that Cummings' success was predicated on the 'frothier' sectors of the FTSE 100, such as retail, house building and commercial property, no one seemed to mind too much.

What should have concerned those at the top of the bank and arguably those who regulated the industry, was the way Cummings constructed many of the growing number of deals he was doing. HBOS was effectively taking equity stakes in the companies it lent to, enabling the bank to ratchet up its lending, often at extraordinary multiples, without making any concomitant increase in its capital.

Cummings joined the boards of dozens of joint venture vehicles created alongside a veritable who's who of retail and property tycoons like Nick Leslau, the Reuben brothers and Sir Tom Hunter. That didn't seem to ring any alarm bells either.

Of course, as we all now know, in the game of corporate musical chairs, when the music stopped playing in the global financial crisis of 2008, HBOS was left with nowhere to sit. Out on a limb and totally exposed, the bank came close to collapse. Investments made by Cummings and his colleagues left the bank with multimillion pound losses and £7 billion of bad debts from loans during their stewardship were subsequently written off.[26] In September 2008, with the markets concerned that there was no way HBOS could ever service its massive debts, it was forced into the arms of Lloyds TSB in a shotgun marriage, brokered by the then Prime Minister Gordon Brown.

Cummings' role in the bank's downfall continues to be the subject of much debate. Supporters say he was not alone in failing to recognise how deep the downturn would be but this seems to be missing the point.

The scale and recklessness of dealmaking on the High Street has played a significant role in the sorry state the sector finds itself today. It has been a massive contributor in the erosion and even collapse of many of our household names.

In truth, Cummings was not a lone force seeking out and making extraordinary deals. Prior to the credit crunch, there was a period of around ten years when there was an absolute frenzy of dealmaking in the retail industry. In the rush to make a quick buck, or two, no one seemed to stop for a moment to consider the long-term consequences for this often fragile sector.

What seemed to set it off was the success of private equity deals in America from the turn of the millennium where there was a real boom in leveraged buyouts. There, a combination of decreasing interest rates, loosening lending standards and a harsher regime of rules and regulations for publicly traded companies in the wake of corporate scandals at Enron, WorldCom and Tyco among others, made private equity ownership more attractive. As more and more leveraged buyout deals got done over there, UK companies decided to get in on the action.

[26] http://www.dailymail.co.uk/news/article-1145647/A-660-000-pay-man-broke-HBOS.html

Unfortunately for the long term health of the High Street, each of the deals both here and across the Atlantic followed an eerily similar pattern, known affectionately in the trade as 'slipping and flipping'. Private equity companies would circle public companies, looking for the weakest ones in the jungle, and snap them up for a song, financing the acquisition with a large amount of bank debt. Immediately the deal was signed, the company would be broken into two parts. One part would be 'PropCo', which would inherit all the freehold properties of the acquired company, along with any other useful assets. PropCo then rents back all of its properties to the other company, OpCo, under lease with the promise of upward-only rent reviews to come. OpCo will by now have very few to no assets and will be laden with debts.

The next stage in this scenario is to operationally gear OpCo, which in layman's terms means that as much cost as is humanly possible is stripped out of the company. People are fired, stock run down, trading terms are changed, anything to 'improve' the company's performance. Once OpCo shows a short-term increase in profits, it is swiftly sold, netting the investor a tidy sum, not forgetting that they still have all the crown jewels in PropCo.

In the pre-credit crunch boom years, deal after deal like this were done in the retail industry. The sector featured in the top five destinations for buyout firms every year since 2005. There was a peak of 23 buyouts in 2007, with an average transaction value of £822 million, including the largest ever European private equity deal, where US venture capital giant KKR, together with an Italian entrepreneur, bought Boots the chemist for £11.1 billion.[27]

So far, the Boots story has had a happy ending and trading profit have risen steadily, with the chain reporting over £1 billion in profits for the year 2010/11. In truth, it was always too big and too dominant and there was plenty of fat to cut off from its time in the PLC environment and in particular from its sprawling Nottingham headquarters. However, for countless other High Street names caught up in the frenzy of acquisitions and subsequent slipping and flipping action, the result has been catastrophic.

---

[27] Source: UK Unquote

Why? Because leverage is toxic. The soaring value of UK store chains bought in this way was entirely based on a false premise, thanks to the fancy deals done by Cummings and some of his chums. Crucial retail valuations relied on easy lending from banks and massive operational cost cutting – something which we now know was built on a house of cards. And, as I found at The Big Food Group, it is virtually impossible for what is left behind to operate under a cloud of debt.

More than 150 major retail chains have collapsed since 2008[28] and a great many of these closures were a legacy of buyouts and fancy financial deals done in the boom years.

Take fashion chain Peacocks, for example, which went onto administration in January 2012. When this chain failed, it was carrying debt of more than £1 million *per store*. Half of that debt was secured at an interest rate of 17 per cent. Delve back further into history and what do you find? There was some financial footwork that put the company under a great deal of pressure, to say the least.

Chief executive Richard Kirk sold half his holding in the retailer for more than £13 million in 2006 while leading a management buyout which loaded Peacock with high interest borrowings. The transaction, backed by a consortium of private equity houses, valued Peacock's share capital at £404 million, at a time when the group had about £70 million of net debt.[29]

After the deal, the retailer's borrowings jumped to £460 million as it absorbed the costs of the buyout – some of which was at that incredible annual rate of 17 per cent. In the following years, Peacock's liabilities soared while trading conditions worsened for the entire High Street as the economic slow down took hold.

The inevitable happened. The retailer simply could not support the debt and after the shock of the credit crunch, banks are no longer as willing to bail out indebted companies.

---

[28] Source: Real Business: Trouble on the High Street, 9 February 2012
[29] http://www.guardian.co.uk/business/2012/jan/20/peacocks-collapse-rocks-retail-industry

Peacocks is not alone. There are many, many more privately backed retailers which, if they haven't done so yet, will go bust in the coming years, crumbling under the weight of their debt.

It's not just the private equity firms that are benefiting out of all of this either. It can prove quite a draw for those at the top of retail businesses who stand to make a penny or two out of agreeing to a good deal taking their company private.

Retail businesses are notoriously undervalued by the markets. When you are close to a business and know what it is worth, it can be pretty frustrating to see the low value the markets put on your stock. You'd have to be a pretty strong-willed individual to resist the potentially huge personal payout if the company is taken into private hands.

I'll put my hands up here and admit it; I too got tempted by just this scenario while I was at Wickes. It was a few years into the turn-around following the fraud case. We'd done a rights issue in 1996 and started implementing a five-year recovery plan which aimed to rebuild our relationships with employees, customers and suppliers, improve margins and build the Wickes brand. We'd also kicked off Project Crystal to invest in a new store format.

Considering the hand I'd been dealt, it was all going pretty well. Except it was only me and my colleagues who seemed to think so. The markets remained stubbornly unimpressed and the share price remained at rock bottom.

Sitting in my office one day with finance director and good friend Bill Hoskins, I told him what had been troubling me for some weeks.

"If this is all the shareholders think of our company, maybe we should just buy it ourselves," I said. "It's got to be worth looking into, at the very least."

Of course, even just 'looking into' a management buyout is a very difficult thing to do when you are a chief executive. Clearly, the moment you begin considering such a strategy, you are not acting in the best interest of your shareholders. There is a conflict of interest. If an MBO begins to looks like a real possibility, you have to resign at the earliest opportunity.

All the same though, it was a pretty tempting proposition.

Bill and I talked it through and agreed that we owed it to ourselves to at least give the idea the once over. We resolved that we would talk to one private equity house and if they said they were not interested in backing it, we would let the idea drop. We both had a job to do at Wickes.

For two weeks the pair of us worked day and night to hone our presentation. When it was just right, we took it along to the private equity firm Apax to see if they wanted to back our deal. They turned us down flat though, so we didn't make an offer.

The reason they didn't chose to back us are lost in the mists of time, but I suspect it was something to do with a keen ex-retail fellow the firm had just taken on. Well, he had a retail background but judging by the nonsense he wrote about our pitch, he really didn't know what he was talking about. But, that is the way things go and, as we had agreed, Bill and I returned to Wickes to continue what we had started in the turnaround.

The story didn't end there though. Our view that Wickes was undervalued was utterly vindicated when, just a year after our presentation, rival DIY chain Focus Do It All swept in with an opportunistic bid. The privately run Focus chain was 59 per cent owned by Duke Street Capital.

Bill Archer, Focus' chief executive, initially approached me with a 380p a share offer, but when we turned that down as laughably low, he was so infuriated that he tabled a hostile bid at just 375p a share.[30]

It was obvious that this bid did not recognise the value and potential in Wickes, as Bill Hoskins and I knew only too well. Archer saw, just as we had done a year earlier, that the company was grossly undervalued.

[30] http://www.guardian.co.uk/business/2000/mar/31/9

I had no option but to fight back and make sure the company was not bought for a song and ended up in the midst of a bitter, two-month long takeover battle. There were many moments when we thought all was lost – particularly when Archer managed to convince one of our largest institutional shareholders Schroders to sell him a 20 per cent stake at 430p per share – but Bill Hoskins and I managed to get the other major institutional shareholders on side after an exhausting round of presentations. Eventually good sense prevailed and we won, staving off the hostile bid.

Although this outcome was a source of huge personal satisfaction for me, particularly as any hostile bid situation inevitably gets extremely personal and a lot of muck was thrown over those months, what happened next is what is most significant in the story of retail's financial house of cards.

After the bid had gone away, I took some time to take stock of the situation and work out where to go next. It was a buoyant time for DIY chains, with home makeover TV shows such as Changing Rooms riding high. My gaze fell on Homebase, which was at that time owned by the supermarket giant Sainsbury's. Homebase has traditionally sold a mix of goods at the lighter end of DIY, such as lighting, fabrics and soft furnishings, whereas Wickes specialised in the heavier stuff, such as tools, materials and building equipment. It seemed to me that the two companies would compliment each other perfectly and executed properly, a combined Wickes Homebase group could be a real credible rival to B&Q. It could offer DIY goods at the hard and soft end and attract customers of both sexes and from all sides of the DIY spectrum.

As luck would have it, at that moment Sainsbury had just taken on a new chief executive, Sir Peter Davis, so now seemed a great time to see if he wanted to offload their DIY business. Sure enough, Sir Peter agreed to a meeting and the pair of us met in secret at one of Sainsbury's company-owned flats in the old GLC building by Westminster Bridge in London. At that meeting, we agreed in principle to a deal.

I decided that, if a deal could be done, this would be the time to take the company private too. Events of the past year had done nothing to change my mind that Wickes was undervalued and no one seemed particularly interested in our stock. That left me with two things to do. I had to find a backer and I also needed to see Duke Street Capital. Duke Street and Bill Archer still owned 27 per cent of my stock, built up over the takeover bid, so they would need to be on-board with any bid for Homebase.

As it turned out, finding a backer was the easy bit. KKR were keen to get involved and we lined them up almost straight away. Duke Street, on the other hand, said they would only come in on it if Focus was included in the deal, making it a Wickes, Homebase, Focus conglomerate.

After all I had been through in the past few months, I dismissed this scenario out of hand. There was no way I could work with Focus.

So, the deal fell through.

It was now obvious that Wickes was never going to be able to take part in the large-scale restructuring that was going on in the DIY industry, well, certainly not in the way I had envisaged. With Focus holding on to a large part of its shares, my hands were completely tied. I had little choice but to agree to sell the company to Focus – although I did have the satisfaction of securing 495p for our shareholders just months after seeing off a bid of 375p.

What was not so satisfying was watching what unfolded next which turned out to be a classic example of the worst excesses of slipping and flipping. After buying Wickes, Focus and Duke Street bought Great Mills for £285 million in quick succession the following year[31]. Then, in 2002, Duke Street sold a minority 28.9 per cent stake in the combined venture to Apax for £340 million[32]. A number of the best stores from the Focus and Great Mills portfolio were rebranded as Wickes.

In December 2004, builder's merchant Travis Perkins bought Wickes in a deal which valued the company at a massive £950 million, just three years after Focus had paid £300 million for pretty much the same thing. At this stage, Archer and Duke Street took huge dividends from what was left behind, loading Focus with debt in the process.

[31] http://www.telegraph.co.uk/finance/4474601/Great-Mills-goes-to-Focus-for-285m.html
[32] The Independent

Within months it became apparent that what was left of this DIY group couldn't operate under the weight of the debt. By 2006, it emerged that the group had come close to breeching its bank covenants and was struggling to pay the interest on its debt. A slowdown in the DIY market did not help matters much, but it was obvious to all concerned that things could not go on. In June 2007, US hedge fund Cerberus bought Focus in a deal that valued the struggling company at £225 million. The public owners of £100 million of mezzanine debt in the company got just 40p in the £1.

It is here that I came back on the scene, working with Cerberus to restructure the group. But, despite my best efforts, Focus could not be saved. It collapsed into administration in May 2011.

Much of the soul searching that followed the demise of Focus concentrated on the shared payouts of almost £1 billion taken out of the chain in over a decade of dealing and financial engineering. According to analysis by The Observer newspaper, Duke Street Capital, which made an initial investment of £68 million in 1998, took £700 million out of Focus in a series of capital and debt restructurings that turned the once small, Midland-based chain into a DIY giant with sales of £1.5 billion[33]. The deal which carved out Wickes from the equation, and ultimately left the rest of the group struggling, also netted Apax a healthy profit.

Yet, away from all of the head scratching over how this can happen and the natural revulsion at City fat cats, there is another very important factor to consider; the human cost.

More than 3,000 shopworkers lost their jobs when the administrators were finally called in at Focus. Many others were made redundant in the preceding months as we desperately closed underperforming stores in a bid to rescue the whole group.

That story has been repeated time and again elsewhere too. Every time a retailer is forced to close after being loaded with impossible

---

[33] http://www.guardian.co.uk/business/2011/may/29/focus-diy-collapse-sparks-anger-private-equity-firms

debt by their private equity backers, the people who work there are casualties. In the example of Peacocks, which was cited previously, around 9,600 people were affected. Part of the group was subsequently sold to Sun European Partners, but hundreds of jobs still went as a result of what had gone on in the past. Lingerie chain La Senza went at almost the same time as Peacocks, in December 2011, taking with it 2,600 jobs[34]. It was yet another victim of over-indebtedness. There is a long list of failures and every time a store group goes, jobs are lost. Since 2008, more than 150,000 retail jobs have gone, many as a result of leveraged buyouts.[35]

So, next time you read breathless tabloid reports about City tycoons with their lavish parties and multimillion pound yachts, spare a thought for the shopworkers that have lost their livelihoods thanks to the financial chicanery of their paymasters. The majority of shopworkers don't earn much more than the minimum wage and will hardly have had the opportunity to save a nest egg to cushion them against sudden redundancy. For many shopworkers, losing their job has a devastating effect on their household economies and puts many families into real hardship. If they hail from an area where jobs are scarce the situation is even worse because it can take months, even years to find work elsewhere.

Then there is the effect on retail suppliers too, many of which are small businesses. These are the sort of companies that are supposed to be the so-called backbone of the UK economy, yet for them, there is very little protection. In the case of Focus, small businesses were left high and dry with losses of £40 million for goods they had made and delivered, yet never got paid for. It is not an isolated incident.

Plus, we should also spare a thought for the loyal employees who have worked for retail businesses in the past and retired in the 'safe' knowledge they have a company pension to cushion their old age. With a long list of creditors, it is not always possible to pay even secured ones in full when a business goes into liquidation.

[34] http://www.dailymail.co.uk/news/article-2078121/Lingerie-retailers-La-Senza-administration-putting-2-600-jobs-line.html
[35] Source: Real Business: Trouble on the High Street

The question we should all be asking ourselves is what do these deals do for retailers? Or even the economy as a whole? Apart from making a handful of people so rich they couldn't possibly spend it even if they lived 200 years, what has all this financial wizardry really achieved? Has it improved the High Street in any way? Is there any evidence that individual stores groups have prospered and improved under private ownership?

The overwhelming reply to these questions must surely be that in almost every case, leveraged buyouts simply puts chains at a massive disadvantage. Even if shops manage to survive after being loaded with masses of debt, it is unlikely that they will have enough cash to innovate and invest. The best any seem to do is stand still and standing still is never an option in this business for long. It leaves stores wide open to being overtaken by other, more nimble, operators and the next inevitable step is cost-cutting, store closures, job losses and yet more unsightly gaps on the High Street.

The other scenario to consider is: what happens to these store chains after they have been slipped and flipped and sold on to an eager buyer expecting all sorts of magical things promised by the balance sheet? The answer is, they almost never quite live up to their promise.

Take, as an example, Homebase, the DIY chain I had my eye on way back in the year 2000. After being thwarted in my approach, it went to private equity group Permira in December of that year in a £750 million deal[36]. Almost immediately when that the deal was completed in March 2001, it sold about 30 of Homebase's larger sites to rival DIY chain B&Q for £224 million and started to significantly cut costs[37]. Just 20 months later, in November 2002, Homebase was sold to GUS for £900 million, bringing the investors a return equivalent to about six times their original stake. The audaciousness of the deal even won Permira an award for 'Deal of the Year' in the 2003 private equity industry awards.[38]

[36] Retail Week
[37] The Times
[38] http://www.starting-a-business-guide.com/in-december-2000-the-private-equity-house-permira-surprised-the-business-community-when-it-announced-a-buyout-of-the-struggling-diy-chain-homebase-from-j-sainsbury.html

Had Homebase really improved that much in less than two years? Arguably, it was a lot leaner and fitter. By trading it hard, the venture capital backers managed to get profits up from £26 million to £105 million. Had the business substantially changed though? It could be argued quite strongly that it hadn't.

What happens next is interesting. For the first couple of years Homebase delivered for its new owners. But the chain seemed to rapidly lose its shine and from then on in it went rapidly downhill. By April 2009, Home Retail Group (as GUS had become) wrote more than £600 million off the book value of Homebase, revaluing it at more like £250 million while warning that profits are likely to continue to fall. The revaluation prompted The Telegraph to observe: "Private Equity 'gifts' may be best avoided".[39]

To be fair to Permira, Home Retail Group did very little to help Homebase live up to its £900 million promise, whether or not this was indeed possible. In the years it has owned it, Homebase has changed very little. It is still a DIY group, with a green and orange logo, it is still aimed at the softer end of the market and, apart from that, and the addition of many Argos ranges, it has hardly changed.

Meanwhile, Home Retail Group has allowed rival homewares retailer Dunelm to come out of nowhere with an enticing range of kitchenware, bedding and rugs and steal Homebase's customers from right under its nose. Dunelm saw sales up almost nine per cent in the later half of 2011, while Homebase saw like-for-like sales decline by more than six per cent in the same year.

Arguably though, even though Home Retail Group did very little with their prize, would they have ever been able to realise the enormous value Permira placed on it? Probably not.

Either way, the whole thing turned out to be a bit of a mess.

So what of the future? OK, we are still to deal with the companies that limp on after the deals of the boom years, but after the shocking

[39] Private Equity 'gifts' may be best avoided, The Telegraph, 29 April 2009

events that surrounded the global financial crisis, have audacious private equity deals gone away? Not a bit of it. In fact, all the evidence suggests that the High Street is once again a favourite target and deals in the retail arena are hotting up once again. In 2010, for example, more than ten per cent of private equity transactions were in this area[40] and there is no sign that the appetite for retail deals is slowing down, or that they are getting any less ambitious.

In January 2010, for example, pet store Pets at Home was sold for almost £1 billion, following a fierce bidding war between private equity houses. In March 2011, mobile retailer Phones4U was sold to BC Partners in £700 million deal[41] and a few weeks later the sale of Hobbycraft sparked yet another private equity bidding war, this one won by Bridgepoint Capital in a £100 million plus deal[42]. The list goes on.

Investors continue to be highly attracted to the highly cash generative nature of retailing, plus, of course, their strong asset bases. Their modus operandi hasn't changed either, along with the worst instances of slipping and flipping. It is inevitable that yet more retailers will buckle under the weight of toxic debt. Rampant over indebtedness will claim ever more retail scalps and those gaps on the High Street will just keep on widening.

The worrying thing is, matters are just going to get worse too.

The austere, economic climate is making things a lot tougher for High Street chains. The public is a lot more cautious with their hard-earned cash and there are no signs that this will change any time soon. In the boom years, companies laden with debt were at least given the small lifeline of being able to trade their way through it. Well, enough to keep their heads above water, anyhow. That isn't an option today.

Profits have to be cut to the bone today, just to survive. Plus, suppliers, many of which are those small businesses which are the backbone of our economy, are being squeezed even harder to get the best possible terms. Retail chains of any sort of scale are using what muscle they

[40] Source: Retail Week
[41] http://uk.reuters.com
[42] Grant Thornton

have to force their suppliers to cut their own margins to the bone. Of course, the inevitable happens, and many more suppliers will simply collapse under the strain. Supply chain integrity and survival is something all retailers ignore at their peril because, without suppliers they have nothing to sell.

Then, there is the threat of online selling. It wasn't such a big deal early on in the noughties, but now Internet sales are rising in double digits every year. Online sales now stand at 10.7 per cent of overall retail sales[43], equivalent to £573.6 million *per week*. Internet sales will be covered in more detail later in this book, but its role in the fragile financial house of cards is worth mentioning now. With more and more consumers choosing to shop from the comfort of their own homes, it will inevitably put more pressure on chains struggling with extraordinary levels of debts. Paying sky-high shop rents while customer numbers dwindle is just not sustainable. It will lead to ever more store closures as chains close down marginal or unprofitable units and cut back on investing in new stores.

The only chains that will survive in this austere future are those with manageable debt levels, a decent range of well presented and up-to-date stores in the right locations and a dedication to preserving their profit margins. The majority of private equity backed stores simply don't fit into this description.

Ironically, as times get tougher and more and more High Street retailers succumb to the harsh trading conditions, there will be many more bargains on offer for private equity shoppers. So the leveraged merry-go-round will continue with a handful of clever men and women making more and more inventive deals with an ever-dwindling number of store groups.

Then, one day, the entire house of cards will collapse.

---

[43] Source: Office for National Statistics, February 2012

Chapter Four
Puppets and clowns

Successive governments have failed the High Street by either succumbing to intense lobbying of larger players, or simply failing to do anything very constructive when it is obvious action needs to be taken.

I n the early seventies, when I was still a shop assistant at Bishops Food Stores, an edict came down from the government. Every shop, large or small, had to display the price of its various loaves, from baguettes to wholemeal, on an easy-to-find board.

Now, I am as keen as the next man on transparent pricing, but complying with this rule was next to impossible back then. The UK was in the grips of rampant inflation as the government struggled to get to grips with widespread industrial action and the cost of a loaf of bread could change hourly, let alone daily. Of course, if this edict had happened today, shops could have displayed the price on some fancy electronic board, but back then all we had access to for our displays were large silk screen printed sheets. There are only so many times you can take a black marker to a price list before it starts being an utterly illegible dog's dinner. Even putting stickers over the prices was not the best solution.

Yet, it was my job to try and keep the price list up-to-date and vaguely presentable. As I struggled with this seemingly hopeless task, I can remember regularly thinking to myself: does Whitehall really have a clue what is going on on the High Street? This bread pricing idea seems an utterly ludicrous waste of time dreamt up by bureaucrats who don't get out enough, I thought.

It is a theme I have returned to time and again as my career in retailing has progressed. It seems that whenever the government gets involved in anything to do with the High Street, they either get it laughably wrong, or they are far too influenced by the most powerful store groups and support policies which have catastrophic outcomes for smaller chains. It does not appear to matter what side of the political divide they fall on, successive governments have proved themselves to be either puppets or clowns as far as retailers are concerned. The authorities have played a staring role in the death of the High Street, either through badly thought through policies, or a complete failure to stand up to larger chains.

Take Resale Price Maintenance (RPM), for example. The ongoing confusion over price, which followed its abolition in 1964, is what led (at least in part) to the daft edict over bread pricing. More importantly though, the government's decision to bow to pressure and end RPM opened the way for the rise of supermarkets and transformation of the High Street. Or should that say, the beginning of the end for the High Street?

Let's start with a bit of a history lesson, for those who can't remember RPM.

RPM is where a manufacturer and its distributors agree the price at which goods would be sold and the idea behind it was to protect small stores from unfair competition from larger retailers, which could discount goods, thanks to their economies of scale. The logic was that it ensured a fair return for both manufacturers and distributors, and of course, protected the little guys. There were a few official inquiries into it over the 1920s and 1930s, but the governments of the day repeatedly decided not to interfere with the freedom of businesses to sort out their own contracts.

Back then though, the major chains which dominate our High Streets today had not really got their act together. Yet. But, they were already starting to flex their muscles. In fact, retailers such as Marks & Spencer, Woolworths, J Sainsbury and Tesco were getting pretty good at vying for shoppers' hard-earned pennies on the basis of selling the odd bargain here and there. The only problem was, RPM represented a firm impediment to across-the-board discounts. Any retailer that tried to undercut this cosy pricing arrangement would swiftly find their supply abruptly cut off.

Opponents of RPM became increasingly vocal as the last century progressed, not least Jack Cohen, who founded Tesco in 1919. An innovative retailer, Cohen was building up a substantial empire of grocery shops based on the premise of 'a good deal'.

By 1956, thanks to sustained and highly vocal lobbying, the scope of RPM was reduced considerably but this was still not enough for its detractors. In early 1961, Cohen stepped up his campaign to get rid of it altogether. By this time Tesco had more than 185 stores and had just opened its largest most comprehensive store yet, a flagship shop in Leicester which offered a restaurant, a car wash, a filling station and a Home 'n' Wear section selling good value clothes. The supermarket was so substantial that it entered the Guinness Book of Records as the largest store in Europe. Tesco needed a steady, and growing, number of punters to come through the door and that meant it had to tempt them in with cut-price offers.

In an early example of the potential of supermarket power, the authorities quickly capitulated in the face of some pretty robust lobbying. In 1964 the Resale Prices Act declared all resale price agreements to be against the public interest.

The repercussions of the abolition of RPM were breathtakingly quick. In 1959, multiple grocery retailers, such as Tesco, Sainsbury's and Fine Fare, accounted for just ten per cent of grocery outlets and 25 per cent of grocery turnover. A decade later, in 1969, supermarkets had increased their share of grocery turnover to 41 per cent. Today, Tesco alone has a 30 per cent of the market share[44] and one pound in every seven spent on the UK High Street goes through its tills.

It wasn't just supermarkets that were the beneficiaries of the demise of RPM either. The most recent proof of just how much consumers have embraced price and discounting on the High Street, is the rise and rise of pound stores. Pound shops have almost doubled in number in the past decade and very often, when a smaller retail chain closes, it is a pound store which slips in to take its place on the High Street. Indeed, in 1999, there were 380 shops with the word 'pound' in their name. By the end of 2009, that number had increased to 742. Those figures do

---

[44] TNS

not include single-price retailers without pound in their name, such as 99p Stores, which has grown from three outlets in 2001 to more than 125 today.[45]

Along the way, this emphasis on price has had a massive influence on the way we all shop. People used to be quite snobby about where they shopped and we all valued good customer service, but now it simply doesn't matter as long as the price of goods are rock bottom. People of all social backgrounds go to pound shops and seek out offers from supermarket giants and it is seen as savvy and clever to find a bargain. Price, price, price is the mantra of modern shoppers. (This would be great if the bargains on offer were always 'bargains', but we will come to this later in the book.)

As a retailer, I am full square behind the abolition of RPM, because the prospect of having controls over where you can set your retail prices is abhorrent to me. However, it is hard to come to anything but the conclusion that the government's abolition of price resulted in supermarkets flexing their buying muscles and promoting their cut-price goods to such an extent that it led to the closure of thousands of stores. After all, the figures speak for themselves. In 1960, 80 per cent of the grocery market was controlled by 1,621 buying points, yet, by 1970, just 647 buying points controlled the same proportion of the market.[46]

It is no surprise that the government goes to great pains to court the big players in the retail sector; that is how politics works. The search for power and influence always unites politicians and the nation's biggest businesses. Major players such as Tesco, Sainsbury's, Walmart, John Lewis and Arcadia employ hundreds of thousands of people and are vital cogs in the economic wheel. The chief executives of these firms are in and out of Downing Street all the time. When I was the boss of The Big Food Group, which at that time was the fifth largest food distributor in the UK, I too was invited to a reception with the Prime Minister and Chancellor of the Exchequer, as well as to sit on a government committee. The political elite made it abundantly clear that they were interested in what I had to say.

---

[45] Experian
[46] Economist Intelligence Unit 1971

It's a two-way dialogue too and just to make sure, the retailers are active employers of lobbying firms to get their points across to the leading political groups. In 2011, for example, retailers retained 24 lobbing firms, organising a total of 91 Government meetings to discuss everything from energy and climate change issues, to occupational pensions[47].

It is worth it too because, as we saw with RPM, things do get changed if enough pressure is bought to bear. Once you get the government on side, there is very little ordinary citizens, or even smaller businesses, can do to fight any perceived injustices.

I had my own experience of just how impossible it is to fight against the weight of big business concerns back in 2001. Back then, I was chief executive of The Big Food Group and searching for a way to grow the chain and get it on a firm footing.

After a lot of research, we identified convenience stores as the way we could take the business forward. We had the Iceland chain, which were small and medium sized stores located in mainly convenient town centre locations and a food wholesale distribution service in Booker serving thousands of independent retailers. The plan was to rebrand the Iceland stores into Premier, which was the convenience chain of independents that Iceland had acquired with Booker in the year 2000, and use the powerful Iceland brand on a range of frozen foods which we would market elsewhere too. We would then build Premier into a country-wide convenience chain through owned and franchised stores.

I already had had some experience of what worked and what didn't in the convenience market. Earlier on in my career, while at Budgens, I had been made managing director of a small company it had acquired called John Quality. My brief was to convert half a dozen shops into a trial convenience concept. After a lot of research and experimentation, we came up with a format which was called Zipin.

---

[47] http://whoslobbying.com

Looking back now, Zipins were very similar in style to the Tesco Express format, which followed some years later. They sold a range of goods in three main categories: emergency purchases for when you run out of flour or cornflakes, impulse purchases for when you absolutely must have a Snickers and the basic confectionery, tobacco and newsagents (CTN) products which everyone would expect. Zipin turned out to be a hugely successful format and when we built up a dozen of them, they were snapped up by the American chain Circle K.

Some years on I could see that, despite attempts made by Circle K and its American cousin Seven Eleven, no one had really cracked the UK convenience store market and the sector was wide open for a big brand to take it on and build it up. Aside from Circle K and Seven Eleven, which confused the matter by selling coffee and donuts to bemused British consumers (this was in the days before coffee chains stores took over the world), most convenience stores were independent retailers owned by sole proprietors. Although some stores had grouped together to form larger buying groups, there was no strong, unifying brand to capture the public's imagination. It was easy to see there was huge potential in this market.

After spending around half a million pounds on Pricewaterhouse-Coopers research, I went to the banks. In a detailed presentation, I told them that The Big Food Group was going to be a fully integrated food group, with a convenience store twist, that would eventually have a chain of 2,000 convenience stores across the UK. They clearly liked what they heard because they agreed to back us and from then on it was all systems go.

Then, barely a month after the banks had agreed to back The Big Food Group plan, I awoke one morning to the most extraordinary news. Flicking on the radio as I prepared to go into my office, I heard that Tesco had bought the 850-strong T&S convenience store chain for £530 million[48]. At that time Tesco, which had 28 per cent of the grocery market, had built a chain of 100 small Tesco Express stores on petrol forecourts. But this deal, at a stroke, gave it hundreds of stand-alone One Stop and Day & Nite stores across the UK.

[48] Financial Times

I was utterly astonished. How could the government let this deal go ahead? Surely it flew in the face of every single anti-competitive rule out there? For as long as I could remember, 25 per cent was the threshold which signalled a monopoly, yet here was a company which was already three per cent over that and just about to pocket a further 1,000 stores. If The Big Food Group's plans had gone ahead, we would have at best had three or four per cent of the market.

I wasted no time in making my strong feelings against this deal known and I wasn't alone in my howls of protest. The Association of Convenience Stores, which lobbies on behalf of small stores, also complained and called for an immediate Office of Fair Trading (OFT) inquiry. Amazingly though, this notion was turned down flat. The OFT declared that convenience stores were a different sector entirely from supermarkets, despite the fact that people bought exactly the same litres of milk, loaves of bread and bars of chocolate in both 'types' of store.

The whole industry was shocked by the development and no one could really understand why the government was being so accommodating to Tesco. I remember standing up at a conference organised by industry magazine Retail Week and telling the assembled throng that if they wanted to wake up in a world where the choice was Tesco, Tesco or Tesco, they were heading firmly in that direction. We all had to work together to support fair competition in the market, I exhorted. Although I got a standing ovation for my sterling speech, that is as far as it went. People simply didn't seem willing, or able, to stand up against the industry giant.

In the end, after sustained lobbying from a handful of campaigners, including a legal challenge, the OFT backed down and referred the sector to the Competition Commission for a full inquiry. But, after a two-year probe, the competition watchdogs stuck stubbornly to their previous argument that one-stop grocery shopping and top-up shopping at convenience stores are two entirely separate markets. The result? Tesco, and Sainsbury's which followed in its wake, now both have a sizeable chunk of the convenience store sector, to add to their domination of the rest of the grocery market.

This should never have happened. This is not just sour grapes because my own plans for The Big Food Group fell by the wayside. The full-scale assault on the convenience sector by the supermarkets has been to the detriment of the whole sector and hundreds of independent stores have gone to the wall because of it. Between 2001 and 2005, there was a net loss of 2,760 independent stores, a rate of almost 700 per year[49]. This is not to mention the fact that communities have a lot less choice. In some areas, such as Bicester, for example, you are never more than a few hundred yards away from a Tesco. The chain has six stores there, or the equivalent of one for every 4,800 of the population of the Oxfordshire town[50]. Whatever measure you use, this is not fair competition.

The only reason that this happened was because the larger chains have the power and the voice to make people in Whitehall sit up and listen.

It's not just Tesco either. The High Street has been constantly blighted by knee-jerk government reactions to pressure from larger retailers. The abolition of Sunday Trading is another prime example.

Prior to 1994, shops were strictly limited in the hours they could open, thanks to the Shops Act of 1950. It was not a universally popular directive, as can be seen from this fictional comment from a British Army officer in a French novel published around the time of the Shops Act: "If England has not been invaded since 1066, it is because foreigners dread having to spend a Sunday there."

Over the years there had been 26 attempts to relax the laws which saw shops close at 5 p.m. most days, early on Wednesday to 'borrow' time to stay open longer on Thursday and then completely on Sundays. The various attempts to change the rules met stiff resistance from trades unions, religious groups and even, at one time, some larger stores such as Marks & Spencer and Waitrose. The pressure to change was, in the main, supported by larger chains who lobbied hard for the

---

[49] OFT
[50] http://www.telegraph.co.uk/news/uknews/1540392/Bicester-the-town-Tescod-six-times-over.html

change, often flagrantly ignoring the law in their efforts. Margaret Thatcher tried and failed to quash the law, famously suffering her only parliamentary defeat in her lengthy term as prime minister, eight years before the UK Trading Act was finally passed.

I was working in Hong Kong when this happened, but the negative effects on some smaller businesses as a result of relaxing Sunday trading were rapid and continue to be marked.

It's not over either. Under the current rules, shops larger than 3,000 square feet are restricted to just six hours of opening on Sundays, a time limit most are not happy with. However, the Government suspended the regulations to allow shops to open longer hours during the 2012 London Olympics. It is thought to be only a matter of time before the time limit is got rid of altogether which will be yet another victory for the lobbying power of the big retailers and yet another nail in the coffin for small independent stores.

The Association of Convenience Stores said in 2005 that liberalising Sunday Trading had already had an adverse effect and any further relaxation of the rules could see 30 per cent of smaller retailers shut down and 44 per cent cutting jobs. That is, of course, not to mention the knock-on effect on family life. Britain is already at the bottom of the table in Europe for evening and weekend working, with one and a half million parents working weekends – a time when children are not at school. After what has been allowed to happen to date, it is highly likely that the Sunday Trading rules will soon become a thing of the past.

This type of scenario happens time and again. History shows us that all too often, the government of the day swings too far in the large retailer's favour after enormous pressure is brought to bear. The flip side of this is when it does so by default by simply failing to do anything very much when it is obvious action needs to be taken.

The best example of this is the successive Competition Commission investigations into widespread and repeated complaints that supermarkets are manipulating prices and treating suppliers badly. The first of these inquiries, in the year 2000[51], found that the big five supermarkets Asda/

---

[51] 'Supermarkets: A report on the supply of groceries from multiple stores in the United Kingdom.

Walmart, Morrisons, Safeway (which has since been taken over by Morrisons), Sainsbury's and Tesco did indeed hold 'power' over the market which might act against the public interest. For those who made the complaints, it seemed like a good sign when the Commission was particularly vocal against the pressure put on suppliers to keep prices low, or even sell goods at below cost, which as well as crippling their business, meant they were likely to invest less and spend less on new product development. This meant less innovation, lower quality and less consumer choice declared the Commission.

In a further positive sign, the Commission was also critical of practices such as 'price flexing' where large superstore prices were set according to local competitive conditions, rather than on the basis of costs. So, if there was no competitor they would charge as much as they could get away with, regardless of the impact on poor communities.

Yet, inexplicably, despite all the evidence and the damning report, the Commission recommended next to no remedies, declaring the market was 'generally competitive' despite the weight of evidence to the contrary. The only recommendation which came out of this first inquiry, which was then passed on to the OFT to implement, was for a code of practice for the treatment of suppliers. From the very start, the idea of this code, which was to be drafted in conjunction with, and then policed by, the supermarkets, raised a few eyebrows among the suppliers it was supposed to protect. After all, what supplier would be brave, or foolish, enough to put their hand up and say they were not being treated fairly? It is odds on they would never get a contract again after complaining, and with the big five dominating the bulk of the market, it would be commercial suicide. The grocery giants had suppliers in an armlock and everyone could see it, except the authorities which were meant to make sure such unfair practices were not allowed to happen.

When the Code of Practice finally appeared in March 2002, it was worse than anyone had imagined. Indeed, after being watered down so heavily by the supermarkets, it was virtually worthless. Supplier groups, such as the NFU, which were consulted over the draft, condemned the final version.

The Code never stood a chance of being effective and made no difference whatsoever to the way suppliers were treated. But, of course, no one complained. Suppliers vented their frustration in anonymous letters written to the industry magazine The Grocer, but that was as far as they dared go. One said they couldn't do anything because "I would get blacklisted immediately"[52]. Another said it could not go to the OFT because it would "damage the business even more"[53]. In a Friends of the Earth survey at the same time, a third of respondents who experienced problems said 'fear of delisting' was their reason for not complaining.[54]

Whichever way you look at it, the role of the government's official regulator's as guardians of the public interest fell woefully short in this episode. Their soft stance towards the larger retailers opened the way to them getting bigger and more powerful, to the detriment of the rest of the High Street. But this was just the beginning. The authorities had another chance to put things right just a few years later and failed again dismally.

Fast forward to the year 2006 when the government was still under intense pressure to do something about the growing dominance of the supermarket giants. After a series of legal challenges, the Association of Convenience Stores won an appeal against the OFT and forced it to take action.

This was the cue for a number of heartfelt appeals from the industry, which showed that the situation on the High Street had dramatically deteriorated in the short time since the authorities last failed to do anything.

Brendan Barber, the General Secretary of the Trades Union Congress, gave evidence that "below cost selling is having an even greater effect now than in 2000", and the National Farmers Union reported an increasing number of complaints from its members. Suppliers, many of them speaking anonymously, told of pressure to pay to 'win' contracts with supermarkets, or of across the board price cuts with little

---

[52] Code is an 'irrelevance', The Grocer, 15 February 2003
[53] Safeway extracting every last penny, The Grocer, 15 February 2003
[54] Farmers and the Supermarket Code of Practice, Friends of the Earth, 17 March 2003

warning and no discussion. There were stories of demands that suppliers agree to exclusive agreements with one store group, or even of being forced to pay the difference when retailers failed to meet profit targets.

After a gruelling two year investigation, during which it received 700 submissions from retailers, suppliers, consumers and local authorities and held 81 hearings across the UK, the OFT did concede it had found evidence that the 'buyer power' of the major supermarkets had increased since the earlier report[55]. But, despite the weight of evidence to the contrary, it insisted consumers were benefiting from the rivalry between stores and smaller shops were 'not in terminal decline'.

"It is not impossible for them to compete and in the current economic climate the benefits of vigorous competition are as relevant as ever," the report said[56].

The report was dominated by proposals for changes to the planning system, which would make it harder for one chain to monopolise a local area and there was a recommendation for a new, tougher Code of Practice. In a bid to prove that this Code of Practice meant business, there was a recommendation for a new independent ombudsman to resolve any disputes and assuage any fears among suppliers that they will be delisted if they speak up. The ombudsman would be given the power to 'levy significant financial penalties' on any large retailer which did not comply with the code.

It was a great start. But, four years on, very little has happened. To begin with there were some strong challenges from retailers, who issued stern warnings that consumers would pay the price for an ombudsmen. Then, Tesco challenged the proposed competition test for planning, which resulted in the government watering down some of the requirements.

The new Code of Practice finally came into force in February 2010, declaring that practices such as altering supply terms retrospectively,

---

[55] www.competition-commission.org.uk
[56] Competition Commission; The supply of groceries in the UK market investigation, 30 April 2008

or asking suppliers to fund promotions, was outlawed. However, as the National Farmers Union pointed out at the time, this was not a whole lot of good without an ombudsman to enforce the rules.

It wasn't until May 2012, after almost a decade of campaigning by suppliers, that the Government has finally agreed to put in place a supermarket watchdog to ensure fair treatment all round. The idea of a Groceries Code Adjudicator (GCA) was announced in the Queen's Speech on 9 May, but at the time of writing there are still no clear indications as to whether the adjudicator will be able to fine stores which fall foul of the code, or indeed how much power it might have. There have already been mutterings among the industry that it could be a 'toothless watchdog', while the British Retail Consortium is already fighting back warning the GCA will make it harder for retailers to invest, grow and create jobs.

The other side of the coin to the Government's apparent inability to withstand the pressure of big retailers, or lack of resolve when it comes to cracking down on obviously unfair practices, is its laughable attempts to go solo and 'help' the High Street. This is the 'clown' part of the puppets and clowns story.

Take free parking, as an example.

"There is never anywhere to park," is a continual refrain, whenever people are asked about the woes of the High Street. And, in a lot of ways, they are right. Parking, and plenty of it, as any retailer will tell you, is the lifeblood of the business. But successive governments have managed to completely cock up parking provision and charges, thus forcing people away from vulnerable town centres.

It all started with the national green agenda in the eighties and nineties which sought to encourage us out of our cars and onto public transport. The authorities pushed up town centre parking fees and the number of available spaces that could be added were sharply curtailed. Of course, the average consumer clearly thought that that green initiative must be meant for someone else and simply got in their car and went to shop in the by-then burgeoning out-of-town centres with their plentiful and, more importantly, free parking. The more expensive and hard-to-find town centre parking became, the more we all got into our cars and went elsewhere. Indeed, some estimates suggest that 60 per cent of motorists now drive further to out-of-town shopping centres simply because parking is easier.[57]

Even as far back as 1996, 83 per cent of businesses warned they believed the planning system for major projects was too bureaucratic in design and implementation[58], yet very little has been done by central government to encourage local authorities to reverse this badly thought through policy. There is simply no impetus to give stronger consideration to the impact of parking provision and charges on the already beleaguered High Street. At the same time there is very little incentive for local authorities to do much to change the status quo, because sky high parking charges have turned into a useful revenue stream.

In many ways, it may even be too late to change things anyhow and it hardly looks likely that many councils are about to start offering free parking for all (although it has been trialled in some areas and proven to produce a marked upswing in town centre shopper numbers).

Perhaps cash strapped local authorities missed a trick in the rush to grant permission for out-of-town centres over the past few decades. They could have put conditions on the gigantic car parks that went with them, saying retailers had to charge motorists for parking there and pass a proportion into council coffers. Of course, they can't do that retrospectively, so instead they are left charging ever higher fees in town centres. Meanwhile, more and more shoppers drive further afield.

It's not just big policy changes where the government spectacularly fails to see the bigger picture on the High Street. Very often, even the timing of various announcements seems to completely misjudge the way retailers work. Witness the VAT hike on 31 December 2009, from 17.5 per cent to 20 per cent, the night before most shops start their January sales. It is undoubtedly the busiest and most stressful time of the year and that is before you even consider the monumental task of

[57] RAC
[58] British Chamber of Commerce Report 1996

changing all in-store signage and labelling for an ill-timed tax change. Hardly surprisingly, it was an utter fiasco and caused real disruption to the sector. Many retailers even resorted to putting their prices up well before the end of the year, some as early as November, so the poor consumer got some really bad deals in the run-up to Christmas that year too.

The Government showed a similar lack of understanding of the retail industry when it walked into a furore over VAT on hot food, with the so-called 'pasty tax'. The move, announced in the March 2012 budget, declared that all food sold 'above ambient temperature' must now carry 20 per cent VAT. VAT is not charged on most food and some drinks, described as zero rated, but will now be payable on takeaway food sold to be eaten hot.

Many fast food retailers met the decision with a combination of protest and derision, not least because there is no real definition of that temperature. If you are selling a pie which is 22 degrees internally on a hot sunny day, does this mean you don't have to charge VAT on it? What if there is a sudden squall and the mercury dips below 18 degrees? Does that mean you have to rush to add 20 per cent VAT on at the till? It just doesn't make sense. Although the Government has subsequently backed down on this, it is just yet another sign that it really does not have a clue about what is happening on the High Street.

The latest well-meaning intervention from Whitehall concerns new rulings that retailers have to keep cigarettes hidden from view. From April 2012, all shops in England which are larger than 280 square metres have had to install new units which will cost an estimated £15.6 million. Smaller retailers will have to follow suit in 2015.

It's all laudable stuff in the battle to get smoking down and to stop young people taking up the habit. However, retailers argue that when the same government departments that introduced these new laws are still considering the possibility for plain packaging for all tobacco products, these new cabinets could well be an expensive irrelevance. The cabinets simply don't make sense until a full decision is made on plain packaging.

Even the Government's much-publicised 2011 review on the High Street is ludicrously misguided. Although the Conservative Government is to be congratulated for finally listening to what most people have long been saying – that the High Street is on its knees – who did they bring in to examine what could be done about it? Mary Portas, the so-called Queen of Shops. While there are plenty of seasoned retailers who have long lived and breathed the real problems of the High Street and its every twist and turn, the Government chose to bring in a TV retail personality to get to the bottom of this weighty issue. Granted, Portas has early career experience of working on window displays for Harrods and Topshop, and as a creative director of Harvey Nichols, but the bulk of her career has been as a PR and brand consultant, as well as a TV presenter. Arguably, it might have been a whole lot more effective to get a bunch of seasoned retailers and planners together to thrash out what could really be done for the long-term viability of our town centres.

While in many cases retailers have not helped themselves, what cannot be ignored is that interference by the government has not furthered the cause of the High Street and in many cases it has actually damaged it. A combination of badly thought-out policies and a complete failure to act against clearly unfair practices have seriously impaired its chances. Plus, the successive governments have been consistently too willing to be swayed by the most powerful store groups.

At the root of the problem is the fact that there is little real incentive for any government to act decisively to protect the long-term future of town centres. Most politicians think in terms of one term of parliament, perhaps two if they are really forward-thinking, but the problems the High Street now faces need real, long-term, vision if we are to end up with any half-decent solution. On current and historic showing, we shouldn't be looking to Westminster to provide the answers.

Chapter Five
Property Lemmings

What we have seen so far is just the beginning. There will be more and more empty shops on the High Street as retailing polarises into a handful of super-sized shopping parks.

I n my early twenties I enrolled in a night school course at Slough College to do a diploma in management studies. By then I had decided that I was in love with the buzz of retailing and was absolutely committed to a lifetime in the sector. Now I was determined to climb the career ladder. So, by day I got hands-on, practical, experience as a trainee manager at Bishops Food Stores and by night I worked hard to learn the theory behind leading a team.

Towards the end of the course, I joined my fellow students on a four-day residential session in Oxford. The main focus of this intense period of study centred on something that was ominously called 'the lemming exercise'. The lemming exercise was a simulation of the growth and development of a fictional white goods business over a five-year period. After dividing up into teams, our challenge was to nurture our fledgling businesses, while at the same time taking into consideration the various macro and micro economic influences which were periodically introduced and highlighted by the tutors who were running this course.

Although I was the youngest in my particular team by a street mile, in fact I was the youngest on the entire course by a long way too, in typical confident-Grimsey style, I immediately adopted the role of leader.

In a gung-ho and motivational speech, I told my 'colleagues' that we needed to adopt a strategy for growth.

"In five years' time, this company is going to be the market leader, no question," I told them confidently.

We got off to a cracking start too. Within a year, our stock price was sky high and business was booming. Even as other teams fell by the wayside and went belly up in the early years, it seemed like nothing could stop us. At the halfway stage, our imaginary business was far out in front of the rest of the pack and apparently going strong.

Then, towards the end of year four, my business imploded.

In our race for growth, I had failed to heed the warning signs that the economy and selling environment was changing and that I needed to adjust the strategy accordingly. I had blindly pursued what was initially a successful plan, but failed spectacularly to come up for air and look at the bigger picture. I hadn't taken enough account of all the macro and micro clues that were being fed to us by the team.

To salvage a little pride, I might add that my business was the last to go out of all the ones involved in the exercise. Plus, it is not known as the lemming exercise for nothing. The tutors were putting forward extreme economic factors to test a business to its limits and no one was expected to survive the full five years. But hey, my wonderful business was no more and it was a great way to learn some important lessons.

The reason I relay this tale now is because I can see a lot of parallels between this lemming exercise and what is happening to the property side of the retail industry today. People are not taking into account the bigger picture.

In all the soul searching and discussion about disappearing stores and what is happening to our High Streets, very little, if anything, has been said about property, apart from the fact that there are an awful lot of empty shops. Yet, what is happening right now in the retail property market could have a more devastating effect on our High Streets than anything else that has gone before. Like the lemmings in my college exercise of 35 years ago, we are collectively heading for a massive fall, but no one seems to have noticed. Plus, and this is the really interesting bit, the implications will be far more wide reaching than anything that has gone before. The current property trend could wipe out many of the out-of-town shopping malls and retail parks that have contributed so effectively to decimating our town centres.

In some ways it is strange that property has thus far been largely left out of the 'death of the High Street' debate. For most mainstream retailers, property has always been one of the most essential parts of their business. (This is obviously changing with the growth of the Internet – but I will come on to that shortly.) Indeed, bar employees, bricks and mortar are one of the biggest expenses that any retail organisation faces and a misjudged rental or leasing agreement really can make or break a retailer, even a large one.

The pace of change in retail property over the past 40 years has been breathtaking. Since I first began as an apprentice butcher's boy, shops have steadily got larger and larger. One of the most vivid memories of my early career was back in the early eighties when Tesco opened one of its first superstores in Neasden, north London. I was working at Budgens then, which had recently bought my old company Bishops Food Stores and I was the only director they decided to keep on. Having made me fresh food director, the Budgens CEO recommended that I checked out Tesco's new store to see what they were up to.

When I saw the Neasden Tesco, I was utterly gobsmacked. Up until then, stores of 10,000 to 20,000 square feet were considered large. This was a 50,000 square foot giant of a store. I remember catching my breath as I walked through the automatic doors and thinking; this is huge. It is like an aircraft hanger. I couldn't imagine what they could possibly fill it with.

By today's standards, 50,000 square foot is now considered pretty small, although the Neasden Tesco has undergone several expansions and now boasts over 100,000 square foot of retail space. But it is not the largest store in the portfolio. Indeed, Tesco's largest store, in Walkden, Greater Manchester, boasts a breathtaking 185,500 square foot of shopping space. Since the early eighties, supermarkets have just got larger and larger and they have filled them with an ever wider range of products from clothes, to toys, to home furnishings. Some chains had even added in mezzanine levels to eek out even more selling space.

It hasn't just been supermarkets that have been swelling up like no tomorrow either. Just a mile or so up the road from Neasden, where I first saw that giant Tesco, is Brent Cross, the site for the UK's first stand-alone shopping mall. The futuristic concrete block may not be to everyone's taste today, but when it opened its doors in 1976, it was a sensation. From its glamorous indoor fountain, to its promise of a new, American, shop-till-you-drop culture, it was something shoppers had never experienced before. Even those in the supposedly cosmopolitan Capital were used to strict 9.30 a.m. to 5.30 p.m. opening, with early closing at least one day a week in most stores.

The naysayers who dismissed Brent Cross as a white elephant couldn't have been more wrong. It was the mall which kindled our love affair with dedicated shopping enclaves and spelled the start of a frantic building boom. In less than 40 years, there are now around 900 shopping malls, from small local centres, to gargantuan gilded shopping malls such as Westfield in London's Shepherd's Bush, with a retail floor area of 1.615 million square feet, the equivalent to about 30 football pitches and Liverpool One, with 1.4 million square feet, the size of 14 football pitches. Together, all these huge shopping emporium offer more than nine million square foot of shopping space across the UK, which equates to 17 per cent of retail space[59].

Retail parks, those large outdoor lots, criss-crossed with cavernous brand-named warehouse-style stores from B&Q to TK Maxx, have multiplied at an enormous rate too. There are now more than 1,485 of them, either established or in construction, and in the past ten years the total capacity has grown from 147 million square foot, to 176 million square foot[60].

And people love them too. Over 2.4 billion annual visits are made to shopping centres across the UK and the average group spend in out-of-town centres is £55, compared to £34 in town centres[61].

Looking at these statistics alone, it is easy to see how some town centres have been casualties in this race for growth. The property boom of the eighties and nineties means there is far more shopping space than we need. Property developers and retailers became too greedy

[59] BCSC Retail Property Statistics
[60] The Definitive Guide to Retail and Leisure Parks, 2012, Trevor Wood Associates.
[61] BCSC Retail Property Statistics

about putting too much space down and went too far, creating far more than we ever needed. It is a simple case of supply and demand. There is, after all, only ever so much shopping that can be done, but faced with a choice of a glitzy new mall and a dying town centre dotted with empty, boarded-up shops, it is pretty clear where people will choose to go and spend their money. You can organise as many town centre 'market days', or community events, or pop-up shops as you like, but in the minds of the public, it will never compare to the easy accessibility, free parking and broad assortment of stores offered by purpose-built out-of-town malls and retail parks. We've all moved on too far, and experienced too much, to accept anything but the newest and 'best' experience.

You can't blame the shopper. Now the retail industry has ignited their appetite for a 'shopping experience' they are becoming more demanding by the year. They want shopping malls and parks with the full complement of popular shops such as M&S, John Lewis and Next. However, now that spark has been lit, even that is not enough. Mere shops are no longer all we desire to keep us all happy and spending our cash. There is now a growing demand for other forms of entertainment to enhance the experience too.

Just ten years ago, leisure facilities accounted for just 2.5 per cent of floor space and five per cent of spending. Today, in newer shopping malls, those figures have quadrupled to ten per cent and 20 per cent respectively.[62]

We've come to a point where no developer in their right mind would design a new shopping centre or retail park without some sort of leisure offering such as restaurants, a cinema, a bowling alley and whatever other modern distraction is needed to keep consumers amused.

The trouble is, the 'best' experience changes all the time. One new, more glittering, more exciting mall and retail park has superseded the other. Yet, the sad inevitability is that each new wave of retail development simply swallows up – and spits out – what went before it. What is left behind are dismissively called 'secondary' sites and generally fill up with

---

[62] The Definitive Guide to Retail and Leisure Parks, 2012, Trevor Wood Associates.

a depressing mix of pound shops, coffee bars and down-at-heel chain stores which can't afford slots in the bigger malls.

There are clear signs that property companies are struggling to fill vacant units in centres which were only built a handful of years ago.

Many of these now vacant shops once housed retail casualties such as the now defunct Land of Leather, MFI and Rosebys and my own former venture Focus. Indeed, I can remember a time when Focus was the last man standing in one empty and windswept out-of-town centre in Blackburn. Everyone else who had been on the site had either gone bust, or moved to busier, more lucrative, locations. Needless to say, we weren't seeing much footfall there.

It is a vicious circle. Consumers are not willing to make the journey to run-down, out-of-town centres, or retail parks, or secondary malls, with a less than full complement of shops. The greatly reduced footfall drive the shops that can afford it to move into more popular parks, leaving the ones that are left to struggle even more as they become increasingly isolated. The original area will die a lingering death as one store after another leaves.

So, what of the older out-of-town shopping centres which exploded onto the scene in the eighties and nineties, which don't boast all these bells and whistles? The very centres that were blamed for kick-starting the death of the High Street? Well, in a fantastic twist of irony, they will rapidly go the way of the town centres which they helped to destroy only a short while earlier. The UK shopping and entertainment industry will polarise into fewer and fewer, yet ever larger, centres and more and more communities will suffer.

But, this is not all. It is my contention that the huge shifts in the retail property market, which have been gathering pace over the past 40 years, will pale in comparison to what comes next. The scale of the changes to come will be more extraordinary and more damaging than anything that has gone before.

Our retail environment is facing two major threats. Actually, it is not facing them at all; it is currently slap, bang in the middle of the maelstrom.

The threats are the growing North-South divide and the Internet.

Let's take the North-South divide as the starting point. If you spend any time looking at the retail property market – and as I said earlier not many people do - you will have noticed that the scale of development of these new shopping centres has slowed down considerably. Indeed, the year 2012, was the first year since BCSC (British Council of Shopping Centres) records began in 1983 that there has been no opening of any significant centres.

The sites that are in development are evolving in a very particular pattern. Developers appear to be concentrating on the affluent South-East, with large-scale projects in Croydon, Bromley and Kingston on the drawing board, as well as a redevelopment of that shopping mall pioneer Brent Cross. There is far less activity in the provincial towns and cities and the only two developments of any note in the North of the UK are in Leeds and Manchester.

Why is this? As a rule of thumb, developers have always liked to have at least 75 per cent of retail space pre-let before they commit to a scheme, because they need this guarantee to secure finance for the project. Therefore they work closely with retailers to make sure they are all singing off the same hymn sheet.

Although there is a surfeit of space on the High Street, major retailers are still hungry for more. The trouble is, they want the *right* space. They want bigger and better outlets in high footfall, affluent areas, even though it means they will have *fewer* shops in total. The trend of moving out of quieter shopping malls into larger, busier ones is just the beginning. It is now becoming glaringly apparent that those retailers who can (and these are the ones that hold the power and can sway developers to commit to a project) are abandoning many of the quieter, less affluent, outlets in the North and concentrating their energies into new larger and more lucrative malls in the South.

There is already a noticeable North-South divide in town centres. The average national vacancy rate – number of empty shops – is 14 per cent, but Northern towns make the top ten worst performers[63]. Stockport,

---

[63] Local Data Company

for example, has a vacancy rate of over 30 per cent, while Nottingham, Grimsby, Stockton, Wolverhampton, Blackburn, Walsall and Blackpool all have vacancy rates of over 25 per cent. Conversely, the shopping parades of St Albans, Salisbury and Taunton boast a vacancy rate of less than nine per cent.

The High Street's younger cousins, the shopping centres and out-of-town retail parks, are now also showing clear signs of a North-South bias. According to the BCSC, one in five UK shopping centres are at risk and where are the majority of these mainly secondary locations? In the North. Indeed, more than 20 shopping centres are on the market, including centres in Perth, Middlesbrough and Blackpool.[64]

The North, which has already been hit hard by the Government's post-credit crunch austerity measures because it is arguably less equipped to withstand them than the more prosperous Southern counties, now faces the prospect of even further economic struggle as more shops head South. Don't forget either that this isn't simply a case of consumers facing less choice about where they shop. Retail is one of this country's largest private sector employers, giving jobs to 2.9 million people, or one in ten of the working population. Just as much of the turnover in retail is accounted for by a few dominant stores, so are the employment prospects and the ten largest retail groups employ a third of those who work in the sector.[65] If stores migrate South, so do the jobs.

The reasons why large store groups are becoming so ruthless and digging into the best possible retail sites are twofold. The first is the obvious reaction to cuts in spending, as consumers tighten their belts. Every square foot of retail space has to pull its weight and it makes good business sense to concentrate your efforts in the place where you will make the most money. The second reason is down to the relentless growth of Internet shopping. Retailers are only too aware that online retailing could be a powerful enemy that can – and will – take down High Streets, shopping malls and retail parks alike. The more consumers

[64] Call for revaluation of UK's recession hit shopping centres, Graham Ruddick, The Telegraph, 5 May 2012.
[65] Annual Business Inquiry 2009, and Labour Force Survey

choose to shop from the comfort of their own homes, the less viable some of these bricks and mortar places will be.

The growth in online sales has been astonishingly fast. They've doubled from five per cent of retail sales in the year 2000, to ten per cent in 2011 and are forecast to rise to 12.2 per cent by 2014[66]. In 2010, 79 per cent of UK Internet users said they had ordered goods or services online[67] and these same users are more likely to visit retail websites than Internet users in other countries, with 89 per cent saying they did so in 2011.

What does this mean to retailers? In the busy Christmas period of 2011, fashion retailer Next reported an increase of 3.1 per cent in group sales. However, in that period, Next's *store* sales fell by 2.7 per cent. The rise in sales was down to their Internet operation.

If you delve into the figures further, there are some more worrying trends for both the High Street and the secondary shopping malls. If you look more carefully into the figures though, you will see an even more worrying trend for non-food stores. While online sales counts for 11 per cent of total retail sales, within the non-food sector that figure is 18 per cent. That means that for every pound spent on non-food goods, 18p of that is now spent online. Consumers are becoming increasingly more comfortable buying DIY equipment, soft furnishings, toys, electrical equipment and fashions over the Internet.

Now let me share with you a list of the top 20 retail park tenants[68]:

B&Q
Homebase
Currys
Matalan
Next
Carpetright
Comet

[66] Verdict
[67] OFCOM
[68] The Definitive Guide to Retail and Leisure Parks, 2012, Trevor Wood Associates

Argos
Halfords
Pets at Home
TK Maxx
Boots
Wickes
Marks & Spencer
Toys R Us
Dunelm
Harveys
PC World
Dreams
Mothercare World

Although many of the chains on this list have already fought back by launching their own, successful, online operations, there can be no denying that the Internet is putting an ever increasing amount of pressure on their business models. After all, Internet-only operations such as Amazon don't have to worry about paying high leases on onerous terms for a countrywide network of stores. Plus, the cost of starting up an Internet-only retail chain is far lower than for setting up a bricks and mortar operation. The large-scale stores on this list are in constant danger from the next hot new dot-coms on the block, not to mention Tesco which now boasts an online catalogue of 23,000 products. The entire retail environment is changing and it is changing fast.

It's not just the retailers that are under pressure either. The retail landlords who own the shopping malls, retail parks and High Street shops are increasingly feeling the heat too. For these companies, the outlook is more bleaker than it ever has been before.

Being on the back foot is a very new feeling for landlords. In past years, the owners of retail property have always had the upper hand and tenants had very little room to negotiate. The much-criticised upwards-only rent reviews, where rents increase incrementally over periods of up to 25 years, have been blamed for tipping many a cash-strapped retailer over the edge. Yet, the property industry has always been confident that if one retailer couldn't afford their lease, there was always another one willing to take its place. If the shop remained empty (and the outgoing store was not in administration), the outgoing tenant would be contractually bound to pay up until it was filled.

Recently things have changed though. Faced with a battle for their very survival, retailers have been fighting back and there are signs the property industry is, for the first time in years, vulnerable. I first became aware of this when I was at Focus DIY and battling for survival while at the same time trying to pay crippling rents for stores which had long been closed.

Focus was the first time I personally invested my money in a business. Back in July 2007, it was a broken company and US hedge fund giant Cerberus brought me in to take a look. Its previous owners, Duke Street and Apax, had taken a lot of the good sites out of it when they sold Wickes and it was holding a debt mountain of £285 million. I saw an opportunity to turn it around, but not under its then management. When Cerberus asked me to stick around and form a management team, I agreed almost straight away and invested a significant amount of my own money to secure the deal.

In the review of the business, it was pretty obvious that 52 of Focus' 300 stores were not pulling their weight. In fact, they were making a £10 million loss. Closing these stores would reduce our turnover from £700 million to £500 million, but would increase profits from £30 million to £40 million, as long as we got the strategy right.

One of the first things I did on taking over was to bring in restructuring specialists Hilco to dispose of those 52, non-profit making, stores. The shops were immediately hived off into a separate, financially ring-fenced vehicle, owned by Focus and operated by Hilco. Hilco was charged with either selling the stores, or negotiating a way out of the leases with the landlords. Over time, as I made progress with restructuring the group, more stores were added to the list.

Next, I brought in Richard Bird, a great marketer who I knew from my Wickes days, and briefed him to do some research and find a niche that Focus could call its own. In the year that followed, we covered a tremendous amount of ground. We segmented our customers into groups and found our most important customer was the over 55s, or

Arthur and Margaret, as we named them. What interested us about Arthur and Margaret was that they didn't like the ever-increasing size of the majority of the DIY sheds. They had grown just too big. We used to joke that they couldn't even get around the average store without sitting down twice. What Arthur and Margaret craved was a smaller, uncluttered environment, with good personal service, rather like the town centre hardware stores of old.

Our solution was a scaled-down Focus in smaller, 22,000 square feet stores, with a 5,000 square feet garden centre attached. The number of product lines was reduced by almost 30 per cent to simplify the experience and they were to be located in town centres. If there happened to be a large B&Q shed on the outskirts of the town, so much the better because we were confident we would attract their customers on smaller, top-up shopping trips. In many ways, the strategy played to my previous strengths in the convenience market and our early trials gave us many reasons to be confident.

One of the most successful concepts we tried was in Congleton, Cheshire. We had originally asked the landlord of one of our sites whether he would lease us three-quarters of the space because that was all we needed. He came back and offered us half the space. Apparently, M&S was keen to take the other half to open up one of the Simply Food stores. I knew it would be a tight squeeze for Focus, even with their compact format, but at the same time I realised that I would be an idiot to pass up an opportunity to share in some of M&S's footfall. We snapped up the store and did a compact version of our smaller store. Within weeks we were managing to retain the same sales as stores twice the size and make almost double the profit. I felt like I had died and gone to heaven.

Earlier, as I travelled to New York in September 2008 to present my compact store strategy to Cerberus, I believed absolutely that I was on the edge of a revolution in the DIY sector. I was confident that I had found the solution to Focus' problems.

It just happened that the meeting was scheduled for 15 September 2008, the day that Lehman Brothers filed for Chapter 11 bankruptcy and the beginning of a week when the global financial system teetered on the edge. The Cerberus guys, led by tough financier Leonard Tessler, were a tad skittish as I made my presentation because everyone had one ear on what was going on outside in Wall Street, but they listened to what I had to say.

I explained the strategy behind the convenience stores, 'introduced' them to Arthur and Margaret and told them about the success of the pilot project. I said I wanted to roll out a further six stores to develop and test the new format further. I finished my upbeat presentation by reminding them that our rolling credit facility was due to run out in December 2009. Legally, I had to have a new agreement in place by the time Focus filed its accounts in February 2009, because we needed what is known as a 'going concern statement', which showed the company had more than one year's money in reserve.

Although they listened politely and were encouraging about the new format, it was immediately obvious that Cerberus were not about to commit to anything very much in the light of what was going on in stock markets around the world that day. Not only did I not get the go ahead to press on with the convenience store trials, I was also left with no answers on the rolling credit facility.

Things didn't look better once I got back to the UK. Although I tried to press on with things, I still had no clue as to how to solve the finance problem and new challenges seemed to pop up almost daily. Then, just as I was starting to think things couldn't get much worse, Hilco handed back 30 of the stores it had been charged with selling on or negotiating its way out of, blaming the 'change in the economy' for the volte face.

Now, on top of the looming credit facility crisis, I was paying extortionately high rents, service charges and insurance on these 30 empty stores, plus for another eight we had closed in the past few months. It was costing us £12 million a year to rent space which was not generating a penny of income. This was enough to send the company over the edge and I knew it. Even if we could just limp by from month to month, we would never be able to invest in the chain and become a credible competitor to the rest of the DIY sector.

Then, as if out of the sky, the answer appeared. JJB, a struggling sportswear retailer, which had been limping from crisis to crisis, presented its creditors with a company voluntary agreement (CVA) which was designed to offset the considerable costs associated with the 140 stores it had closed in the preceding months. The innovative proposal, which was overwhelmingly approved at a creditors' meeting in April 2009, involved landlords accepting a considerably reduced rent in order to ensure the survival of the company. JJB was able to hand back the empty stores and the onus was then on the landlord to fill the space. This was a 180 degree turnaround from the previous situation where JJB paid rent every month on empty properties, therefore leaving very little incentive for landlords to find new tenants.

"That's it!" I thought. It was exactly what Focus needed to cut it some slack.

A JJB-style CVA was an opportunity to get rid of the liability of Focus' crippling rent outflows on empty stores and would give me leverage on signing a new revolving credit agreement with the bank, contingent on a successful CVA.

A CVA can only be done with 75 per cent of creditor approval, but I would be able to show that thanks to the CVA, and the bank facilities that would be signed on the back of it, the company would survive. If the company survived, it would therefore go on paying full rents elsewhere. Under the alternative, which was for the company to slide into administration, landlords would get nothing at all.

A CVA does not leave the landlords of the empty stores completely high and dry. Although Focus would stop paying rental, service charges and insurance, the landlords received a dividend totalling £4 million. This meant we had saved more than £8 million a year and the landlords still got a nominal sum.

I immediately put in train the CVA and the deal worked like a dream for us giving us some much-needed breathing space. It didn't go down so well with some retailers though. Ian Cheshire, the chief executive of rival DIY chain B&Q, even wrote to landlords demanding better terms following the Focus CVA.

"The system is being exploited by some managers to get rid of what they don't like in one go. It is being presented as 'if you don't agree to this, we'll go bust'," he said at the time.[69]

Cheshire was not alone in his opposition to CVAs. Indeed, the debate over CVAs has raged ever since, partly fuelled by the fact that JJB returned for a second CVA just two years after the first. Since then, a growing succession of hard-pressed retailers reeling from the credit crunch and ever-rising rent demands, have turned to them as a potential means of survival. Blacks Leisure, Stylo, Sixty UK and Jessops are just a few of the names that have tried to go down this route, although not all have been successful in their bid to stave off the inevitable.

Of course, the most outspoken of all against the CVAs are those who stand to lose the most. Retail landlords are increasingly taking a hard line on CVAs, and perhaps hardly surprisingly have began calling them an 'absolute disaster' for the industry as they grow in popularity. After all, CVAs significantly reduce their income with no guarantees that the tenant will survive.

Ultimately Focus was one of the ones which did not survive. With hindsight, I should have been more aggressive with the original CVA and said that not only did I want to hand some stores back, but I also wanted to renegotiate rent on the other trading stores, because the leases there were way too high. In fact, even though I had become non-executive chairman in Focus' final difficult year, I was just working on a CVA2 to do just this, when Cerberus pulled the plug because it was unwilling to put more funds in the company in such a tough market any longer.

Looking back now at the lessons I learned at Focus, I firmly believe that there has to be an informed and serious debate about retail property. The sector has evolved to where it is today with no real discussion or descent, as can already be evidenced by the fact we are sleepwalking into a devastating North-South divide. The property side of things has a staring role in what is going on in the changes on the High Street, but it is rarely even mentioned.

[69] Retailers in battle over JJB closures; Rupert Neate, The Telegraph 12 February 2011

While we've all been looking the other way, rents have been allowed to get ridiculously high and with those wretched upward-only reviews there has been very little that anyone can do about it. Companies such as Focus really did have no choice but to resort to CVAs.

As the pressure on the High Street continues, I foresee many more retailers doing everything they can to reduce their rent burden. If landlords are not more flexible they will simply hasten the inevitable and more shops will disappear for good.

The question is, will retail landlords embrace this trend and work together with stores to find a middle ground? Or, like lemmings, ignore it and continue to play hardball?

Don't forget, it is not just hard-pressed retailers that are eyeing their property costs either. With consumers increasingly turning online, even profitable retailers are looking at sky-high rents and wondering if they might be better off with fewer stores. If the property industry will only but see it, the writing is well and truly on the wall.

At this stage, many people may be thinking; so what? These property giants have had it so good for so long, it is about time they felt some of the pain of the High Street. Sadly, whether you are directly involved in retail or not, the downturn in the property side of things is bad news for everyone.

In the first place, if property companies keep on building newer, better and bigger malls, with little thought to the secondary malls or ailing town centres, the overall situation is only going to grow worse. The retailers that can will simply decamp to the newer malls, while those who can't afford to will wither and die when consumers reject half-full retail parks for better shopping experiences elsewhere.

The physical and psychological effects on communities left with these empty retail spaces will be, and already are, enormous. Empty retail parks and decaying town centres drag down house prices and attract a criminal element.

There is another worrying long-term trend too though, because the property companies behind this are not simply faceless giants who build and manage shopfronts and malls. Their entire financial models affect the pensions and investment of millions of Britons. In short, if they suffer, so do we. In spades.

The key investors in the UK's largest property companies are pension funds. Names such as Aviva, Standard Life, Prudential and Henderson have billions tied up in the future of our High Streets, malls and shopping centres. The investment managers who make the decisions about High Street properties – and who are seemingly ignoring the keys signs that the High Street is changing irreconcilably - may well be betting on our futures. Yet, in all the head scratching and discussion over the future of our shops, nothing is ever said about the potential time bomb our pension funds could be linked with.

The long and short of it is: there is too much retail space. If the current trend in property is allowed to continue unfettered by the larger macro and micro economic indicators, we are all headed for a bigger fall than we have ever imagined. Developers will continue to build larger and larger retail developments, which suck in all the biggest retail names which themselves are cutting down on their total square footage in response to the growth of the Internet. Meanwhile, retailer after retailer will fall to victim to sky-high upwards-only rentals, many of which were negotiated years ago, and most of those that are left will have to do their best in what's left of High Streets or older, less-fashionable retail parks. It is only a matter of time before the UK, and in particular the North, is pockmarked by empty retail parks and malls, alongside abandoned town centres. When the whole merry-go-round stops playing, it won't just be landlords who will be left holding these empty properties. It will be you and me through our greatly diminished pension funds.

At least my lemming exercise was imaginary. What is happening in retail property now will have a long-lasting effect on all our futures.

PART TWO

What does it mean to you?

Chapter Six
Have we now got the High Street we deserve?

We've all played a role in the demise of the High Street, thanks to our relentless quest for lower prices and convenience. While we happily looked the other way, we handed too much power into the hands of too few retailers.

In 1988, I went to Hong Kong to run Hutchinson Whampoa's Park 'n' Shop supermarket chain. After a career spent in UK retailing, this was a bit of an eye-opener.

People shopped completely differently there, thanks to the climate and the culture. Back then the shopping experience was dominated by wet markets, which can be a bit of a shock to those of a more delicate Western constitution. The aim of these traditional markets is to show that as much of the produce as possible is super fresh. This means the fruit and vegetables still have earth on them and look like they have just been lifted from the soil. It also means that the meat, such as poultry and fish, is still alive, until it is swiftly dispatched by the market trader, or taken home to its fate by the shopper. The rationale behind it is that buying goods in this way is the best way to ensure against viruses and diseases which breed voraciously in the hot climate.

When I arrived it was immediately clear that the country was in the throes of a change of culture. The younger generation, who had been exposed to television and western movies, were becoming increasingly brand aware. They weren't so keen on the noisy, chaotic, water-soaked, environs of the wet markets. They wanted ordered, well laid-out and sterile supermarkets bursting with brand-named groceries, just like those enjoyed by shoppers in America and Europe.

The trouble was, the supermarkets in Hong Kong at the time were a million miles from this ideal. They pretty much only sold groceries, leaving all the fresh food to the wet markets.

I could sense immediately that there was clearly a demand for things to move on.

Using the knowledge gained from my time spent in UK retailing, I set about transforming Park 'n' Shop into a new breed of supermarket. We built the first, multi temperature-controlled, distribution centre in South-East Asia and began importing brands from all over the world. The centre included frozen, chilled and even tropical temperature-controlled environments with a floor dedicated to butchery and meat packing plants. It was fantastic.

We could pick up cartons of Covent Garden soup from the UK, put them in temperature-controlled transport, and the products wouldn't get one degree hotter in the entire 48-hour journey to the shelf in one of our Hong Kong stores. The large ex-pat population in Hong Kong welcomed this development with open arms.

We changed the layouts of Park 'n' Shop to include far more space for fresh and frozen produce.

Now all we had to do was to persuade the locals to shop there. After all, in a close knit, hierarchical, society like the one in Hong Kong it doesn't matter how much the youngsters hanker after Western-style living, because if their mums or grandmothers don't approve there is little chance of it catching on.

To gain everyone's confidence, we employed the services of the mythical Mrs Wong. The character, who appeared in all our TV adverts, was given film star status as she apparently travelled around Hong Kong in a limousine, regally sweeping in and 'examining' Park 'n' Shop's fresh food deliveries and giving the nod to the warehouse facilities. We ladled it on a bit thick, but the message was clear; this respected local lady approved of what we were doing.

Her notoriety became complete when she appeared in one small screen advert inspecting a line of butchers to check on hygiene. The row of straight-backed butchers, clad in pristine white coats, looking for all the world like soldiers in an army parade, had their cleavers clamped firmly at their side like rifles. In this scenario, the imposing figure of Mrs

Wong immediately spotted a fleck of meat on the cleaver of the last butcher in line and advanced upon him. As the music built, the poor butcher shrank away in fright as Mrs Wong grabbed the cleaver and her shadow advanced towards him. Then boom, the cleaver comes crashing down. The camera pans away to reveal the cleaver embedded in the wall and a shocked butcher breathing deeply as he sinks to the ground. Mrs Wong signed off by declaring that Park 'n' Shop meat was always the freshest, prepared in the most hygienic conditions and no one was left in any doubt. Well, this ad became a phenomenon in Hong Kong because it scared the living daylights out of young children! It generated more publicity than money could ever buy. I wasn't even sad when the authorities finally pulled the plug because it spurred on another wave of banner headlines about Park 'n' Shop.

The ad did its job and the sale of fresh and frozen foods by supermarkets started to become acceptable and our sales soared. Park 'n' Shop, which was turning over £200 million and making £1 million in profit when I arrived, was turning over £400 million and making £20 million of profit by the time I left five years later. I had played a part in transforming the shopping habits of people in Hong Kong.

This story is, I believe, an accelerated version of what has happened to our own UK High Streets over the past four decades, where we have all moved to an entirely different, more convenient, shopping model. Over this time, UK consumers have moved away from the lengthy and frequent shopping trips once enjoyed by my mother Louie, and into giant superstores, shopping malls and retail parks for an entirely different way of buying their goods.

In any analysis of the demise of our town centres, we cannot avoid discussing the role that you and I have played in this trend. After all, while it is very easy to cry "it is the fault of supermarkets/big malls/ out-of-town chains", we are the ones who put money in the tills and therefore, by implication, we chose the tills we put our cash in.

The inescapable fact is this: the reason shops close is because people no longer shop there. Just as in Hong Kong, where young people fuelled a move away from the wet markets, shoppers demanded something different here too.

In chapter one, we briefly covered some of the changes to society which have had an influence on how we buy our groceries. Developments in domestic technology, with increased ownership of fridges played a part in how often we shop and what we buy. So too did affluence, travel and convenience. There are plenty of other factors at work in our shift away from the High Street too.

One of the biggest influences is the fact that many more women work today. In the fifties, only one in three worked, whereas today almost half of the entire workforce are female and they are playing an ever more important role in the workplace too. Yet, whether women are running a company, or simply have a part-time job at a local store, the fact is they no longer have time to painstakingly trawl several different local shops for a range of ingredients to cook the family supper. Time taken in gathering these ingredients is wasted time. It is far easier to buy it all under one roof, or even to buy a pre-made ready meal for the family.

Part of becoming a time poor society meant that many shoppers started to welcome the anonymity and quick service offered by 'modern' supermarkets, rather than the chatty, socialising of local shops that characterised my youth when Louie could spend upwards of 20 minutes in *each* store. Supermarkets, with their self-service operation and super-efficient checkout operators made shopping a practical consideration. Nothing more, nothing less. Shoppers could go in, grab a basket, pick up their groceries and have it whizzed through a conveyor belt checkout in minutes, even when it was one of the older manually-operated tills.

It is hardly a surprise that the self-service business model was seized upon by clothing, leisure and DIY retailers too. Seemingly overnight we all welcomed the notion of picking out our own goods, putting them in a basket or trolley and then whisking though a checkout without hardly giving a shopworker a second glance. Personal service was out. Fast, efficient, contact-free shopping was in.

Similarly, with it becoming the increasing norm to have both adults in the house working, a local store which opens from nine 'til five, with an hour for lunch, just didn't cut it any more. Shops that close just as you are leaving the office are no use to working people. It is little wonder that when push comes to shove most families would rather go to an out-of-town mall at the weekend for their clothes, leisure goods and furnishings, rather than nearby boutiques and town centre stores. Late night opening supermarkets are a godsend too. Throw in an ample supply of free parking and now you are really talking.

Even the old arguments about High Streets being a vital social hub no longer ring true thanks to modern social media outlets. Indeed, there is a generation of people that have never experienced the joy of running into an old friend on a trip into town and stopping for a natter.

"Why would I want to stop and chat on a rain-lashed street, when I can catch up with everyone on Facebook whenever I want," anyone from a younger generation would say.

In truth, while most people pay lip service to the notion of quaint town centres, with a diverse range of independent shops, less and less people have supported them. They voted with their feet (well, wallets to be exact) overwhelmingly in favour of supermarkets, retail parks and big sheds. Then, as one shop after the other closes through lack of custom, the High Streets becomes an even less desirable place to shop, because there simply isn't the range of goods on offer and the situation goes from bad to worse.

It is a controversial thing to say in some quarters, but perhaps it is worth considering that supermarkets and general retailers have merely *reflected* changes in society. They were simply the first to recognise that most of us no longer have the time to potter between the butcher, the baker and the candlestick maker and responded to the different patterns of consumption.

Of course, retailers needed scale to serve this growing market, and that is not always a good thing, as we will come to in a moment, but look what they managed with it. Supermarkets, for example, could answer our need for more variety and convenience because they had the wherewithal to open up huge markets in developing countries for them to export their food. At a time when increased leisure travel took off, and the impact of immigrants on product ranges grew, in the seventies and eighties, supermarkets pioneered the import of goods such as mangos and avocados. They changed our whole perception of what we could put on our tables. I can still remember the joy of anticipation throughout my childhood when the first Jersey Royal New Potatoes arrived on the table every year, after months without them. We'd eat them up with lashings of melted butter and enjoy every mouthful. Then, as supermarkets took over, we could suddenly have new potatoes every day of the year. We could have strawberries, beans and peaches anytime we wanted too. We, the consumer, asked for it and supermarkets delivered.

The trend that supermarkets were best-placed to tap into is the prolonged boom in consumerism. In the past 40 years, there has been a radical shift in our values and, as a society, we now appear to lay more store in the goods we buy, than in the people we know and live alongside. Since 1971, there has been an eightfold increase in spending on recreation and culture. Back then, just six per cent of households could afford the luxury of two cars and nearly half (48 per cent) did not own one at all. By 2007, 27 per cent of households had two cars, while only 23 per cent had no car at all. In the past decade alone, we have gone from 29 per cent of households owning a personal computer, to 70 per cent. Mobile phone ownership has soared from just 20 per cent a decade ago to more than 78 per cent today[70]. Tumbling prices and widespread availability have made goods that were out of the reach of past generations, the norm.

Seeking out and finding luxury goods and bargains is the ultimate in modern self-gratification and this environment has played right into the hands of big retailers. Well-run, international store groups, with their efficient sourcing and lower cost bases, are able to offer the shopper the best possible value. Even if they cannot offer the best price on the High Street (and they don't always do so as we will see in chapter eight), their advertising and promotions will scream that they do, and shoppers will flock through the doors to snap up bargains left, right and centre.

The truth is, the general consumer cares very little for heritage, or sentiment, or picturesque High Streets. If the goods they want to buy are cheaper elsewhere, they will buy them and who can possibly blame them?

[70] Office for National Statistics

According to research, one consumer in five feels no loyalty at all to any particular retailer and views every purchase on its own merits. Indeed, one consumer in ten even looks down on those who are still loyal, viewing anyone who fails to hunt out the best possible deal as a fool.[71]

And, so we come to the question of scale. After all, in order to offer the keenest possible prices, retailers have to be as competitive as possible. What is the easiest way to compete? Well, scale always helps, as does having less rivals.

The tough question we all need to consider is this: in our quest for value, did we allow certain retailers to become too powerful? In other words, have we got the High Street we deserve? Although it would be naive to suggest that the gaps on the High Street are the fault of consumers, we can't avoid looking at our role. After all, we have already looked at the role of the authorities, which have either looked the other way, or been unduly influenced by large business concerns. Perhaps, at the very least, we, the consumer, have a case to answer for being similarly apathetic while a handful of organisations rapidly took over our retail landscape? While embracing the notion of lower prices, little thought has been given the potential downside of too much power being in the hands of too few retailers.

This is not to negate the part played by major store groups. Our retailers operate in a free market where only the fittest survive and grow. They had to go on getting more and more competitive, or leaner, fitter rivals would have taken them out. Top-line growth is what sustains successful retailers. There is, however, a case that says consumers have allowed major chains to become far more dominant than is wise.

In the following chapter, we will see the negative results of allowing too few store groups run the show and how it impacts variety and choice, but first let's take a moment to look at how we all (albeit perhaps subconsciously) encouraged a shift in power on the High Street to answer our growing desire for convenience and value.

---

[71] Store wars and the new consumers, www.mindlab.co.uk

The facts are these. Up until the seventies, the manufacturers of big name brands dominated the grocery market. There was a massive consumer demand for well-known products, fuelled by a multimillion spend on newspaper and poster advertising and on TV when that became more widespread. These manufacturers called the shots, even among the larger retail groups. When the Walls', Kellogg's, or Heinz salesmen visited a store, or a retailer's HQ, everyone from the buyer to the checkout girls sat up and listened. These salesmen were all like peas in a pod, with sharp suits, highly polished shoes and smart briefcases. Retailers did not buy from them; they were told what they would sell, even down to the percentage discount they could offer for a promotion. These manufacturers also used to keep fleets of vans out on the road and, as I described earlier in this book, the deliverymen were the wiliest, most cunning, duckers and divers around.

Although, compared to the big brands, supermarkets had been the underdogs for a while, there were a handful of larger retail businesses who were especially quick to notice changes in society which could be hugely significant. They saw that the rise in ownership of fridges meant consumers did not need to shop as often and that the whole notion of 'lifestyle' was gaining traction, with people travelling more and thinking about the whole notion of luxury and leisure. Shoppers were becoming more au fait with the idea of choice and the fact that they didn't have to always stick to the same menu, diet, or even store. Supermarket chains such as Tesco and Sainsbury's very quickly cottoned onto the fact that once consumers knew they had choices, they could shop where they wished. The problem was, to compete for their attention and offer lower prices and a greater variety, the store groups had to wrestle power from manufacturers. They had to take control of both assortment and price.

Luckily for the stores which began thinking in this way, advances in technology were on their side and arguably it was one piece of technology, no larger than a couple of postage stamps, which changed everything and allowed retailers to finally begin to take the upper hand. That innovation was the barcode.

The barcode was introduced in the United States in 1974 and the first product to feature this groundbreaking technology was a pack of ten Wrigley's Juicy Fruit gum. The idea was introduced in Europe shortly after that, although it was a slightly different version to the American one and was known as the European Article Number. Then it spread worldwide. I was one of the founding members of the Hong Kong Article Numbering Association which was responsible for introducing barcodes to Hong Kong.

The barcode transformed the retail landscape overnight.

Until the barcode, retailers had no real accurate information about what they sold, how quickly they sold it and which brands sold more quickly. The only reckoner they had was a stock count at the end of the day. Clearly, with a large store, it was not possible to do a stock count every day, so it would be fair to say that there was a bit of guess work involved in ordering, stock control and displays.

Once barcodes arrived, it was possible to get instant data capture and this transformed the way stores thought about their stock. More importantly, it was the first time supermarket groups had any real insight into consumer behaviour. Today they have loyalty cards and research to tell them everything about our shopping habits, but back then, it was all a bit hit and miss. It was brands with their huge marketing budgets that knew the what, why and how of the goods we bought.

Those supermarkets who could, used this knowledge to begin to weaken the stranglehold of brands. Of course, it was mainly the larger chains that had access to it, because back then the technology was unaffordable to few but the most successful and affluent groups. I can still remember point of sale capture being installed in Tesco in 1987/88 in what they called Project Checkout. The change was instantaneous. One minute we were all pricing up by hand, with price marking guns, and the next time we looked everything was done automatically and we had more data than you could shake a stick at.

The plethora of data meant that space planning and merchandising became a science in modern stores, where previously it had been an art. Instead of piling cans up, standing back and admiring how well the colours matched, as they had done before, retailers could think about their space in a completely different way. Plus, they could think intelligently about what brands occupied their valuable shelf space. They could start playing around with layouts to manipulate what we bought and to use shelves as silent, yet very efficient, salesmen by placing fast selling lines just below the all-important line of sight, for example. Consumers always gravitate towards products at eye level, so slower moving, high profit, impulse lines could be put there to tempt them. Supermarkets would put products that shoppers would seek out, come rain or shine, further up or down the shelves so they could secure two potential purchases: the shopper's usual choice *and* an impulse buy. Overnight, supermarkets were able to improve sales, and more importantly, profitability in their stores. For the first time ever, brands were on the back foot.

After that, the benefits of technology gained pace. Centralised temperature-controlled distribution became more common, as discussed in chapter one, and the brand delivery vans quickly disappeared from the roads. Then, software programmes such as Space Man were developed for the PCs that proliferated in the eighties. Store chains could dump all their barcode-captured data onto this programme and out popped a planogram of the stores which showed *exactly* where they should put products to maximise sales and profitability. Understanding the consumer and pushing them towards one product or another became a complete industry.

The trend signalled a power shift in who 'talked' to the consumer and influenced what they bought. Retailers even started making their own private label brands to take the manufacturers on, head-on, and once again consumers greeted the move with enthusiasm. Indeed, from a base from of virtually nothing in the seventies, shoppers are increasingly choosing own label over branded goods. The UK private label food and drink market was estimated to be worth £37.4 billion in 2011, a 28 per cent increase since 2006 and the number of own label goods launched each year has now over taken branded goods altogether.[72] A number of big name brands such as Robinsons Jam, Sunlight washing up liquid and Omo have disappeared altogether.

There is nothing wrong in all this, you may say. There is pretty much the same result whether you are cajoled into supporting a big

---

[72] Mintel, Private label food and drink – UK, March 2012

brand by an expensive ad campaign funded by a manufacturing giant, or a bit of clever product development and placement by a canny retail group. Except this shift in power kick-started decades of consolidation in the grocery industry. In a perfect example of the Darwinian theory of survival of the fittest, the supermarkets which were most fleet of foot and the best at recognising what consumers wanted, gobbled up the weaker chains. While we happily shopped at the stores which offered the best selections of goods, names such as Safeway, Fine Fare, William Low, Hillards and Mac Fisheries were bought out and consolidated into ever-larger groups, one by one. The more powerful players have expanded relentlessly, supported by us and our wallets, until there are only four major names left: Asda/Walmart, Morrisons, Tesco and Sainsbury's.

Once these grocery groups were assured of an ever-larger group of consumers flocking to their doors, they started expanding things still further. They changed the shape of stores, adding in mezzanine levels selling non-food stuff such as clothes, DVDs, garden furniture and toys. They added restaurants, pharmacies, dentists and even banks. And still the consumers kept coming.

It has got to the point where the average family thinks nothing of spending the best part of Sunday at Tesco, shopping and rounding it all off with a fry-up in the store café. It's become as much a part of daily life as a trip to the park was 40 years ago.

For a retailer fixated on top-line growth – as we all were and still are – this power over the market presents endless opportunities.

Take, for example, the change in the balance of the relationship with manufacturers. Let me share a story from my time at the helm of Wickes. Part of the recovery strategy in the late nineties was to look very carefully at how we could improve our working capital. Now, the dream for any retailer is to be entirely cash generative by selling a product before they have to pay for it. Just imagine the benefits if a shop could acquire a product, then sell it almost immediately for a mark-up on the purchase price, yet not pay the originator a penny for at least 60 days and then only paying back the purchase price. That is retail nirvana.

This seemed to me to be a very compelling idea and with retailers across all sectors growing in power, I could see it was a real possibility too. After all, suppliers needed us more than we needed them.

The solution we came up with at Wickes centred around our distribution and we came up with a method called intermediate warehousing. At the time we had one distribution centre in Northampton.

After looking closely at our manufacturing base, we could see that the bulk of our products were made in the North, while the majority of our sales were made in the South. In our new strategy, we built a new large distribution centre in Warrington and a smaller one in Hemel Hempstead. Both of these new centres, plus the existing one in Northampton, then held stock from the nearest manufacturers to it, and any stock coming into the UK from overseas would be sent to either Warrington or Northampton.

Orders from each store would be sent directly to the warehouses via point of sale data recorded at the till. Each warehouse would fulfil its part of the order and then send it to the nearest distribution centre to the ordering store for consolidation and delivery.

The key to all of this was Wickes *never owned* any of the stock in the warehouses. It was called consignment stock and ownership only passed from the manufacturer to the buyer (Wickes) once it was picked at the warehouse.

Some of the manufacturers took some convincing to adopt this, but most of them did in the end. How? Because even with Wickes as it was then, in a fair amount of trouble, it was still powerful. We could say: this is how it is going to be. You can choose not to supply us if you like, but then clearly we would go elsewhere for our stock.

My ultimate dream was that we would eventually get to the stage where we didn't even own any of the stock on our shelves in our stores and merely shifted consignment stock. Sadly I wasn't at Wickes long enough to achieve that, but I am in absolutely no doubt that I would have done eventually. Just imagine invoicing yourself on behalf of the supplier when the product is scanned at the checkout – now that would be heaven!

As a retail boss I am not alone in my strategy to get the best possible deal from suppliers. This sort of things goes on all the time, in various different ways.

The majority of consumers have not complained. After all, one of the main benefits of scale in the retail sector, is bulk buying. The more consolidation there was in the industry, the more prices came down. Of course, there is the odd complaint from manufacturers, local suppliers and small producers that they were being ground into the dirt by unreasonable pressure from major retailers, but most consumers have consistently managed to turn a blind eye. As long as everyone carries on getting their cut-price goods at a time and place of their convenience, who cares what has to be done to maintain the status quo?

So, what happens? Supermarkets (those all-powerful groups that are left) and a handful of major retailers keep on growing at a relentless pace.

In recent years, there have been signs of dissent among consumers and the campaigning organisation Tescopoly lists more than 450 local campaigns against new supermarket developments on its website[73]. However, even today where the country's 8,000 supermarkets account for 97 per cent of grocery sales, opinion is divided over new supermarket developments. While there is a fair smattering of communities who fight hard to keep the big corporates out, there is always an equally loud chorus of voices welcoming the prospect of chains such as Tesco and Sainsbury's. For every local protest against new store developments, there are consumers who say; hold on, we do want a superstore here, thank you.

It will be very interesting to see where things go from here. We've already noted the rising impact of the Internet on retailing, in the shape of growing online sales, but the World Wide Web has another important role to play in shaping the future of our High Streets. It offers consumers a voice, so they can stand up, be counted and say what they want from retailers. The question is, do the majority want to say anything, or when all is said and done, is everyone happy with what they have got?

---

[73] www.tescopoly.org

For those who do feel they have something to say, the Internet is a powerful tool when it comes to writing, sharing and networking. There are an increasing number of online forums such as Yelp, Trip Advisor and Reseller Ratings, where consumers can comment on everything from products, to service, to price. The Internet has given everyone the opportunity to organise into cohesive groups and highlight the best – and worst – aspects of retailing. By using sites such as this, everyone has the potential to open up the debate about the power balance between store groups and consumers.

And we need to have this debate. There is an overwhelming sense that although the consumer did indeed want better prices, good value, convenience and all the bells and whistles they have now, not many people have really thought things through. In the rush towards change, the majority have turned a blind eye to the less palatable aspects of overwhelming power in the hands of a handful of retailers. In the following chapters, I will show the results of that power and how major chains don't always operate in the best interest of consumers.

None of this is to say we'd have been better off where we were 40 years ago. We've gone way beyond the idyllic notion of the daily shop in the High Street of my youth and everyone knows that. I am equally sure that the youth in Hong Kong are not enlisting the services of a Chinese Mary Portas to agitate for the return of the old days.

What we have to accept is that things have changed and will do so in the future. The difference now is we, the consumer, have an opportunity, and indeed the power, to shape this future.

The million dollar question is; will we grasp that opportunity? Or, do nothing and see how it all shapes up?

Chapter Seven
The customer is no longer King

Shoppers have willingly sacrificed any claim on good service in exchange for low prices and optimum convenience.

N ext time you are in a supermarket, doing your weekly shop, give some thought to the fruit and veg. Don't worry, this is not the beginning of a nanny state-style exhortation to make sure you get your five-a-day. No, what I would like you to do is to consider for a moment why it is that the neatly set-out arrays of oranges, berries, courgettes and aubergines are all there at the *entrance* of the supermarket. It doesn't matter if you shop in Asda, Sainsbury, Morrisons or Tesco, or any of the other smaller supermarket chains, the fruit and veg will always be the first thing you see.

You, the customer, will dutifully fill your trolley with everything from soft fruit, to tender vegetables and then proceed with the rest of your weekly shop. Up and down the aisles you will toil, piling more and more groceries on top of your fragile fruit and vegetables. At first, you may attempt to balance things around the trolley, so you don't squash your fresh produce, but as the shopping trip goes on, it becomes increasingly more difficult. By the time most people reach the final few aisles, they think "to hell with it" and throw in the last items willy-nilly. All the while they will be crossing their fingers that their fruit won't be transformed into juice by the time it gets excavated from the trolley onto the conveyor belt at the checkout.

It may well be that you are so used to this state of affairs, that you have never really given it much thought. But stop for a moment and consider this more deeply.

Supermarkets spend millions on research. They know more about the contents of your kitchen cupboards than you do. Thanks to loyalty cards and regular customer surveys, they know if you are gluten intolerant, have three children and a dog, and all about your favourite tipple. It is therefore not beyond the wit of man to imagine that they are probably more than aware that putting fragile fruit and veg in a trolley at the start of a shop is not the most practical way forward and not really in the best interests of their customers.

The thing is; they are perfectly aware of this but *they don't care.*

Putting fruit and veg at the entrance to the store serves the needs of the supermarkets. They do it because bright, colourful displays of shining fruit and veg look great. Fruit and veg conjures up images of freshness and quality more than any product and most of it can be displayed in pretty much the way it was harvested (after careful cleaning and polishing of course) rather than in sealed plastic, cardboard or aluminium packaging. Put piles of this produce together and they collectively scream: this store is chock-full of excellent quality, great-looking, food. Practicalities aside, which company wouldn't want that wow factor as the first thing their customers see?

It is for broadly the same reason that stores spread the essentials you always buy, such as bread, milk and frozen peas, around the entire store. The tactic forces you to wander the aisles past all the other products they really want you to buy. It is a million miles away from helping you shop in the way you might probably like.

Supermarkets first started putting these impressive fruit and veg displays at the entrance to their stores in the eighties when they stepped up their strategy to cream off what was left of the business enjoyed by the High Street greengrocer. Back then, there were still around 12,000 independent greengrocers hanging on by their fingertips, but only ten years before there were 29,000[74]. The supermarket's innovative solution to capture the imagination of shoppers, and get everyone to fully commit to buying fresh produce in their stores on a weekly basis, was to offer a completely different layout. Up until that time, fruit and veg had to find its own way by being placed on the same sort of ordinary white melamine shelves which housed the baked beans and ketchup. Naturally, it didn't have much of an impact and some customers ignored it. That obviously wouldn't do in the quest to dominate a sector, so a new method to display fresh fruit and veg was required.

---

[74] www.fooddeserts.org

Tesco was one of the pioneers of a new layout that put the fresh food at the entrance to the stores and it displayed its produce in a market stall-style setting. Fruit and veg was carefully laid out in large green trays and displayed at an inviting 30 degree angle to the shopper. Some of the trays even had green and white canopies over the top to complete the effect.

"Look how fresh and authentic this produce appears," was the message. "It's just as though it was laid out on a genuine market stall."

The idea took off, consumers loved it and the fate of the traditional greengrocer was pretty much sealed. Today there are less than 3,000 independents left.

Ah, you may say, but supermarkets have won that battle. Why not move the fruit and veg further down the store, so the customer can pile up their trolleys better and protect their precious produce? The point is, the people who run and plan supermarkets know what an important part of branding their fresh food is. It creates a great impression about the supermarket and the quality of the goods it sells and does so more effectively than any other type of grocery. For a brand conscious chain, it simply doesn't make commercial sense to move the fresh produce anywhere but the front of the store because it does the job that it is intended to do: it entices the shopper in and gets them to part with their money.

And this is the stark truth about retailing today. Although the modern generation has been brought up with stirring rhetoric about the customer being King, or always being right, this is no longer the case and in fact ceased to be a fact some years ago. While shoppers did indeed experience a brief golden age of customer service in the early eighties through to the nineties, this is now far from the case.

Indeed, although we still all believe that shops are looking after our best interests, the whole notion of first class, modern day customer service only ever had a brief moment in the sun. Even then, it was more about a race to become the biggest chain in the shortest time, rather than anything to do with how we rated our shopping experience.

In truth, every step of your shopping trip is laid out with the intention of maximising the amount you spend, nothing more, nothing less. Supermarkets have got psychological manipulation down to a fine art. They are not for one moment interested in keeping our shopping trips brief, efficient and convenient.

How did all this happen? Once again, it helps to start with some lessons from the past.

In the old days, customer service wasn't some sort of marketing discipline and there were no formalised customer service strategies. Shopkeepers simply had one-to-one contact with their customers and it was a point of pride that people left their shop smiling. A brief chat, a complement and a smile worked just fine.

Then, along came large supermarket groups that were hell-bent on growing as big as they could, as quickly as they could. The concept of efficiency became the most important part of the business and as many customer service transactions as possible were automated. It was hardly surprising that, after a while, customers started to feel like they were a bit of a tiresome burden. Those, such as Louie, that had experienced old-fashioned customer service, put up with it with the polite resignation of that generation 'because it was progress', but there was always an underlying feeling that something was not quite as it should be.

Then, in 1982, Tom Peters and Robert H Waterman published *In Search of Excellence*, which rapidly became a hugely influential business book[75]. Looking at the track record of successful companies, it argued that there were common themes which were responsible for their outstanding performance. Out of the eight central themes of the book, getting close to and understanding the people served by the business was seen to be key to growth. Customer service was important, they argued.

The executives who ran the major grocery chains saw immediately that there was an opportunity here. If they got the customer side of things right, they would be able to increase sales and gain market share

---

[75] In Search of Excellence, HarperBusiness, Tom Peters and Robert H Waterman, 1982

even more quickly. Customer service could be a valuable tool in the race for growth.

However, there was a problem. When you are a small High Street store, it is pretty straightforward getting the team to be pleasant to shoppers. The proprietor is probably on-site, setting an example and good personal service is part of the business. Everyone mucks in and is close enough to the heart of the business to understand that it is the steady flow of satisfied customers that pays their wages. But, how on earth do you get people who do menial tasks in vast, impersonal, supermarkets for around minimum wage to do anything else but glower at shoppers? Back then, no one had even considered the idea of creating any incentive for them to go the extra mile, or to engage with the people around them. It was hardly surprising that, as far as the average checkout worker, or shelf stacker, was concerned, they were just doing a job and a pretty unfulfilling job at that.

For a while there didn't seem an obvious solution as how to solve this weighty problem.

Ian MacLaurin, who had joined Tesco as a management trainee in 1959 and worked his way steadily up through the ranks, was one of the first to recognise that getting customer services right could be a key differentiator for an ambitious supermarket chain. He believed, quite rightly, that the British people saw Tesco as a pile it high, sell it cheap merchant and had no real affinity or loyalty to the supermarket. When he became chairman of the group in 1985 he spent a long time weighing up how to correct this and this is what led to bringing me in in 1987 to the newly created role of customer services director.

I have already described in chapter two how I deduced that a lot of Tesco's problems stemmed from the bully boy attitude of the executives at head office and how I went about addressing that. However, as both MacLaurin and I were both acutely aware, it didn't matter how much smiling and encouragement came from head office. We also needed to engage the 40,000 people who actually worked in the stores at the time. They were, after all, in the front line as the people who our customers saw every day. Like it or not though, they did not have the most simulating jobs. Just telling them to be nice to shoppers was not going to work.

After looking at the issue closely we surmised that there were four key points of contact when a customer visits a store and this is what shapes their experience and impression of the chain. The first is the all-important first impression when someone gets out of their car and approaches the shop. Having a trolley park filled with clean trolleys, a rack fully loaded with neatly set out baskets and the area free of litter makes all the difference.

The second important moment is when a shopper engages with a member of staff, possibly for the first time, and this is when they ask for help in finding a particular product. Clearly a reply which consists of a non-committal shrug of the shoulders, or a bored finger pointing off in the direction of the far horizon, is not going to fill the customer with warm emotions about the store.

Thirdly comes the time when a customer wants to complain. Perhaps he or she has found a foreign object in their groceries, or feels there has been a mistake in the pricing. If the store staff start off from the viewpoint that the customer is probably just trying it on, then things are never destined to turn out well.

Finally, there is the experience at the checkout. A long queue and a surely checkout operator is never welcome at the end of an arduous supermarket trip. Any negative feelings will also be compounded because this is, of course, the moment when the customer has to open their wallet and part with their hard-earned cash. No one wants to pay for a bad experience.

Going through these points of contact, as part of my mission to reform customer services at Tesco back in the late eighties, we defined what perfect would look like for each of the four scenarios. So, for example, if a customer asked where the baked beans were, in an ideal world the shop worker would immediately offer to take them to the aisle in question. On the journey they would engage with the customer by perhaps talking to them about their product preferences, or even the weather. It may sound trite, but if you have ever been in the scenario where the store assistant barely looks up before waving you off towards an unclear destination, you will know immediately what a difference a bit of effort can make.

At the checkout, we wanted the operator to greet the customer and give eye contact. We were not prescriptive enough to say they had to say: good morning/afternoon, sir/madam. That would sound ridiculous and forced. Customers in the North would be far more likely to expect a greeting like "Hello duck", while those in the East End of London would respond to "Hallo love". That was fine. The important thing was that the checkout operator acknowledged the customer in an appropriate way.

Similarly, we looked at the complaints process and put in place a strategy where the store staff immediately embraced the problem and did everything in their power to sort it out for the customer. It didn't matter if the shop assistant thought a customer was trying it on. If that was the case, they should keep their views to themselves. Indeed, we didn't want our staff to even be concerned about it, because if there was a widespread fraud, we would pick that up at head office and deal with it. The important thing was that customers went away with the warm glow that said they had been listened to and that someone within Tesco cared enough to want to sort out their complaint.

We produced a video to explain all this to the team out in the stores and it showed clearly what we were trying to do and why. We worked hard to convey the message that if Tesco did well and pleased its customers, we would all benefit, the company would grow and the whole team would get a share of the success. To add grist to the mill, we added an element of competition into the mix, by saying different stores could compete against one another to be our best performing store in customer services, a discipline which was now very important to us. People who work in retail are a competitive lot, so I knew this would work well and we added a financial incentive by donating a considerable sum to the social fund of the winning stores.

To measure how each store performed, we built a mystery shopper programme of anonymous visits to the stores to check on how they were doing. We produced a 20 point checklist, with five marks for each of the four key points of contact and explained that each store would be awarded a score. We then set about producing a monthly league table of the best performing stores around the UK.

I decided the best people to do the mystery visits in the stores were executives at head office. It was a great way to get them out into the stores to get to know what was going on at the coal face. After all, I reasoned, there is little point making policies and procedures in a central office, if you have no idea of what goes on in the real world. Other head office executives were also sent out into the stores to train the teams, and showed a video about how the executive team were changing and meeting new standards too.

This wasn't a hit with everyone back at Tesco's Cheshunt headquarters and my drive towards top notch customer service did earn me an earful or two. Alan Besbrode, the forthright boss of Tesco's research unit, was one who didn't hold back.

"If you think Dr. Penney is going to Portsmouth, Penzance and Peterborough for your customer service programme, you've got another thing coming, Grimsey!" he yelled after discovering I had simply married up an alphabetical list of stores against a list of executives who I was asking to go on mystery visits.

After sorting out the odd geographical inconsistencies to everyone's satisfaction, I did succeed in mobilising the entire company, including Alan Besbrode who became one of the biggest advocates of the programme. Over the next few months, each store received a total of four visits and the scorecards were then sent to my team and collated.

At the end of the process, I presented the results to a conference attended by every single senior Tesco executive as well as store managers. The reaction was electric. Suddenly everyone 'got it' and better still, there was a real sense of momentum in the stores. For the first time ever, there was a realisation that the reason these head office executives had their good, highly paid, jobs was because of the people who shopped in the stores and were served by our store colleagues. The customers were our ultimate paymasters, not this huge organisation we were all working for. If we wanted to keep our jobs and keep growing, we had to please the customer and now we all knew how to do it. We were also able to prove that customer service is a management controllable variable. The stores with the highest customer service results, were also those whose sales, stock results and absenteeism were the best in the company, proving that the best managers produced the best customer service results.

After the success of the customer first campaign, we introduced the same thing in the interface between the stores and head office. We wanted to create internal customer service standards with store queries, so we started a competition whereby stores ringing in would score head office executives for the efficiency of their response. It was wildly successful. (Interestingly, the winning commercial division, was not headed up by one Terry Leahy. His department came second.)

Tesco, however, was not the only organisation to cotton on to the importance of the customer at that time. Archie Norman and Allan Leighton turned good customer service into an art form in the early nineties at Tesco's rival chain Asda. When Norman took over in 1991, the chain was in a desperate condition after a serious of disastrous management decisions and some badly thought through acquisitions. Norman brought in ex-Mars man Leighton and together they set about transforming the Leeds-based chain.

The pair had a philosophy that good service comes from the heart and that the job of an employer is to create a sense of self-esteem and self-worth among their staff, which would then translate into a good experience for the customer. Norman and Leighton got rid of the 'us versus them' culture, which was prevalent at the chain, called the team colleagues, rather than staff, and empowered them at all levels. Along with bonus schemes that delivered long-term payouts for loyal staff, the chain also introduced a wealth of initiatives, such as shift swaps for parents during school holidays, career breaks and time off for voluntary work.

They captured the imagination of the people that worked for them and created an environment where the staff understood the goals, enjoyed their jobs and cared about the customers. The chain not only recovered, but soared in profitability and went on to be snapped up by US grocery giant Walmart in a £6.7 billion deal in 1999.

Another great proponent of treating the team well in order to get the best possible results for customers is Julian Richer, the founder of hi-fi empire Richer Sounds. Richer believes passionately in giving a 'thank you' for a job well done both in financial terms and with thoughtful perks, such as a day off for an employee's birthday. He also offers a wealth of other bonuses, such as a series of holiday homes available to everyone on the team and trips in the company jet.

I love the idea that everyone shares in the success of the company and is properly rewarded for their hard work and admit that I have copied Richer's ideas shamelessly in many of the companies I have worked in. Making everyone feel like part of a winning team pays dividends in massively improved customer service and this does translate into improved performance for the chain overall. In fact, when we sold Wickes in 2000, everyone had become shareholders through the Long Term Incentive Scheme and everyone shared in the success. Checkout operators received at least £5,000 each from the scheme, which was a substantial percentage of their take home income.

One piece of advice from Richer that I really took to heart was that any customer-facing initiatives have to be taken seriously right at the top of the company. That means, even as chief executive, you have to get in there and get your hands dirty. It's a philosophy I have followed for many years now – occasionally with some amusing consequences.

When I became CEO of Wickes, for example, I elected to spend one week every year working in stores to get a better feel for the business and my first store stint was at its Tottenham branch. I quickly discovered that when working at a DIY store there is a lot more to customer service than leading someone to the baked beans aisle. Invariably, what will happen is that a red-faced and clearly stressed person will come rushing up, wielding a small, broken, gizmo, saying they were fixing x, y or z and this bit snapped off.

"Do you know what this is and have you got a spare?" they will enquire, pleadingly.

It is clearly a lot to expect from a shop assistant earning minimum wage to know the inside workings of a full range of household appliances and I quickly understood that we needed to promote some sort of training programme for our staff. To encourage the team to take advantage of this, we took the already devised scheme where they were paid more if they reached certain skill levels and relaunched it as the number one priority in the business.

While I was mulling this all over in my head, my thoughts were interrupted by a young lady asking if the store had any sharp sand suitable for her child's play area. Having only been in the Tottenham store for a few days, I really didn't know. But, according to everything I knew about good service, I endeavoured to help her find out. We ended up having a nice chat as I found the product for her and loaded it on the trolley. I told her to get the checkout desk to call me if she needed a hand loading it onto her car after she had paid.

The shopper was clearly very pleased and, because I had told her I had only been in the job a few days, she wished me luck in my new career as a store assistant. I don't know why, but I couldn't resist telling her that, actually, I was chief executive of the company. She smiled sweetly and went on her way.

Not long after, I heard a roar of laughter from the checkout area. The sound reverberated around the store for some minutes and it didn't take long to find out what was going on. My satisfied customer had told the lady at the checkout that they had a lovely young man working for them, but they had better watch out because he was completely mad.

"He thinks he is the chief executive!" she said, shaking her head sadly.

I suppose the good thing was, this customer still thought about my store in a good way, even though she was a little unsure of my management methods!

I was not alone in gaining inspiration from Asda and Richer Sounds. Back in the nineties, nearly every store group worth its salt invested heavily in employee and customer service initiatives. For a while, most customers probably never felt so good about their shopping experience.

However, what most people probably didn't realise as they got smiles and eye contact at the checkout was that this be-nice-to-you drive was just another component fuelling the rampant consolidation among retailers. While we were looking the other way and convincing ourselves that the service at large stores was no different from that enjoyed at our local mom and pop shops, those local stores were collapsing in their thousands.

And what happens when there are fewer stores to choose from? There is less competition and with less competition there is less need to be so damn nice all the time because customers don't have anywhere else to go.

OK, this may be a little simplistic and cynical, but a lack of credible rivals does reduce the pressure to spend time and money on pleasing customers.

But, there is another reason that the customer services boom of the nineties has been gradually abandoned: the ever-growing demand for lower and lower prices. The search for a bargain is as old as shopping itself, but in recent years buying goods at the best possible price has become the number one goal across the board, even among the most affluent consumers.

Just take pound stores, for example. The idea of selling everything for a pound, or just under, is a relatively new phenomenon in the UK, with many of the oldest chains only having being around for a few decades. However, after a relatively modest growth until the millennium, their numbers have exploded, and the economic crisis of 2008 has sent their numbers into the stratosphere. At the end of 2009, there were an estimated 742 pound stores in the UK and that number grew to 1,500 by the end of the following year and doubled again by the end of 2011[76]. Linked in with the acceptance of these low cost chains has been

---

[76] Local Data Company

the growth in popularity of so-called hard discounters such as Aldi and Lidl. These no frills supermarkets have seen sales increase by as much as 15 per cent a year, when growth at rivals such as Sainsbury and Tesco remains virtually static.

And, what is the first thing to go when you are all competing to sell goods at the lowest possible price? Customer service.

The emphasis on good customer relations has been systematically forgotten as every chain knuckles down to compete hard on price. As the pressure for better and better promotional deals has grown, the once fanatical focus on pleasing the customer has been quietly dropped. We have now, quite simply, got to a situation where the customer gets what he or she is given.

The interesting thing is no one really seems that bothered. If you asked everyone in a crowded room whether or not they have a story of an experience of awful customer services, dozens of hands would shoot up. Given free reign, there would inevitably be no end of lamenting, whining and ranting. But, if you asked those same people which store they would go to if store A sold a product for £2 with no bells and whistles, while store B sold it for £2.20 with exemplary service in a super-chic environment and I bet 99 per cent of your sample group would be beating a path to store A.

As a retailer, I find it extraordinary how far the pendulum of customer service has swung away from what I knew in my younger days. Everywhere you look it is apparent just how far we have sunk.

Take, as an example, the field of home furnishings. The big destination store of my early adulthood was MFI. Back then, any consumer who did not have much to spend, would always know they were in safe hands with MFI. On offer was a showroom filed with inspirational room sets, which were all nicely laid out. The customer would pick out the wardrobe, or dresser, or whatever piece of furniture it was they desired, buy it on the spot and pick up a flat pack version from the delivery counter downstairs. Yes, there were a few Made For Idiots jokes around about the subsequent struggle to put it together, and the inevitable missing nut or bolt, but it did the job. I was once proud to say that I furnished my early homes with MFI goods.

Sadly, along the way, MFI lost its way and its management made a series of ill-judged decisions. The worst of these strategies was when some bright spark decided that what customers really wanted was for their goods to be delivered straight into the home. Inexplicably, in the nineties, the chain built a massive home delivery centre, stopped keeping stock in the stores and customers were sent home empty-handed to await the arrival of their purchase. Sometimes they had to wait quite a long time and very often the order was wrong when it finally did arrive some weeks later. The inevitable happened, consumers voted on this new state of affairs with their wallets and MFI was no more, limping forward into administration in 2008.

The reason I mention MFI is to compare it with the modern alternative, the Swedish furnishings giant, IKEA. To me, the difference between MFI in its heyday, compared to IKEA today, is the embodiment of where we have got to in terms of modern customer service.

For those of you who have never had the opportunity of shopping in IKEA (and there can't be many of you out there because each of its stores boast 35,000-plus visitors a week[77]) let me guide you through a visit.

For the sake of illustration, let's imagine you are looking for a free standing wardrobe for your spare room. After negotiating the cavernous car park, you enter the store through a vast revolving door and are swept on to the escalator going to the first floor. You are being led onto what the store calls 'the long natural way', which is designed to make sure you see the store in its entirety, instead of going directly to the section you know you want.

So, like a hamster in a maze, you are forced through an endless corridor of inspirational room sets. Don't for a moment even imagine you can pop back to look at something you passed earlier because if you want to do this, you will have to push against the impenetrable tide of other hamsters heading in the same direction. No, if you want to see something you have passed before you have to have strong shoulders, or start again from the beginning.

---

[77] www.ikea.com

If you spot something you want, you have to grab one of the plentifully available pencils and a piece of paper, and note down the reference numbers for your own 'picking list'. In the case of our wardrobe, it may not be simply one number. There will be a different reference for the main shell of the cabinet, one for the doors, one for the door knobs and so on.

Then, after entering the maze once again, you will have to negotiate the rest of the furniture showrooms, before being forced downstairs to run the full gauntlet of the Market Hall which is stuffed full of smaller items lined up to tempt you to make an impulse purchase.

Next comes the self-service warehouse, where our exhausted shopper has to lift down the various components of their purchase from a range of different shelves, at varying and often vertiginous heights, while avoiding other exhausted hamsters who are also struggling to load their intended purchases onto large trolleys. Finally, to add insult to injury, there is a queue at the checkout, followed by a wait at the unloading bay while someone in your party goes to fetch the car.

I tried the experience once and for me it was immediately the case of never again. I know millions of people swear by IKEA's mix of contemporary goods at very low prices, which is why this chain has been so successful, but I for one am astonished that we have been so willing to give up so much in terms of good old fashioned courtesy and customer service.

Ikea is not unique. There are signs everywhere of a complete disregard for what a shopper thinks or feels. Indeed some organisations make no bones about the fact that you get what you pay for. If you want rock-bottom prices, then don't expect any frills they say. The airline Ryanair, for example, is well-known for its low cost, no extras model and it utterly unashamed about it. If you want extras such as taking along baggage, eating or drinking, or even going to the loo, then you have to pay for it. And people accept that and have voted with their wallets to fly with Ryanair, even though its customer service is nowhere near top notch by any measure.

Similarly, we seem equally prepared to put up with organisations that can't even be bothered to lay on real people for us to talk to. I have lost count of the times I have tried to negotiate an endless loop of push button, recorded, telephone messages when trying to sort out a relatively trivial problem with a purchase. You can't help but ponder how quickly a bone fide human being could sort this out, as you listen to the tinkle of anonymous muzak played to amuse the hamsters while they wait. When you eventually get through to a human being, they are based in India. What sort of customer service standard pretends that operatives on the other side of the world could possibly help you?

Another excellent example of what we are losing is the self-service checkout systems that are proliferating in supermarkets up and down the land. Retailers may try to convince customers that they are for their own good and reduce queuing time, but I think we all know the real winners here.

By pushing shoppers towards self-service, retailers can save substantially on their wage bill. Up to six checkout operators can be dispensed with at a stroke and replaced with one supervisor to keep the self-service checkout moving smoothly. You do all the work and the retailer doesn't have to bother with engaging with you at any point in the process. Welcome to the brave new world.

Self-service tills are the antithesis of everything customer service should be about. What they say to the consumer is; if you want lower and lower prices, to hell with good service. In fact, to hell with any sort of service at all, because as anyone who has tried one will tell you, these gizmos are hellish to use. First of all it's impossible to find the barcode and even when you do find it, it is often difficult to scan it. Then, when you put through an age-controlled product like wine, or a knife, lights go off and you have to wait for a supervisor to amble over and check that everything is above board. If that is not bad enough, the poor customer has to put up with being barked at by an electronic voice throughout the entire experience.

It's not just the supermarkets either. Other retail genres are getting in on the act and the self-service checkouts which are springing up in DIY stores across the UK have an added layer of frustration. Here, customers are forced to grapple with tiny hand-held scanners while searching for barcodes on large, unwieldy, goods, such as planks of wood or doors, which have been placed on huge, badly packed trolleys. It's a recipe for disaster if ever there was one.

Yet, in our tacit acceptance of all of this, the message is clear: society has apparently decided that what is most important is money – to hell with the experience.

Retailers will retort that such initiatives allow them to pass on savings to customers in the form of lower priced goods, but have we got to a point where we should be asking ourselves just how much we are prepared to give up for a few pence off? (This is to pre-suppose that the savings are all actually passed on which, as we will see in the next chapter, is not always as clear-cut as it might be.)

There is also a further casualty in the get-what-you-are-given shopping culture we have so readily accepted in the race to get better and better deals; choice. The major retailers, and in particular supermarkets, specialise in high volume, fast turnover, goods which they can source in bulk. Every product must justify its place on the shelf by selling in high numbers and selling fast. Thus, in books, chains such as Tesco and Asda stick to the top 100 bestsellers, or even just the top 50. In wine, only the fastest selling, popular wines from well-known vineyards are listed. The same goes for DVDs, magazines, games, medicines, furnishings and electrical appliances. There is no room on the shelves for slower moving lines that hang around for months on the off chance that someone may covet them. That's not how it works. The rule is the same in all aisles – from electrical goods to clothes, to books and furniture - one size fits all.

Yet, if you are that someone who may covet that wine from a lesser known vineyard, or that classic, but obscure, novel your friend raved about, your choice about where you may go to acquire it are greatly diminished. For, while we all shopped slavishly at these large chains in the search of a bargain, the very shops which would have sold you something different from the norm have withered and died.

We are systematically seeing less and less choice of goods on offer and manufacturers, wine producers and publishers have a diminishing incentive to promote new works or produce new products. The question we should all be asking ourselves is; why were we all so prepared to swap service for a lack of choice? Because that is, in effect, what has happened. We've been chasing the pound for so long that we have not really paused to see what we have been left with. When we do finally ask what has happened to choice and customer service, it will be too late. Like the fruit and vegetables at the bottom of our weekly shop, these disciplines have been diminished beyond saving.

Chapter Eight
Not so special offers

Consumers have lost their bargaining power and are now prepared to accept what special offers they are given – even when most of the time the offer is not so special.

These days when you walk into any supermarket, general store or fashion emporium, your senses will be assaulted by wave upon wave of promotional offers vying to capture your attention. Brightly coloured red, orange and yellow signs will declare an item as 20 per cent off. Another sign will scream that this product is on SPECIAL OFFER, while if you buy this one over here, you could get three of them for the price of two. It seems that every inch of space is taken up with material that is designed to persuade the shopper that they are getting a bargain. No opportunity is missed to grab their attention.

Knowing just how much the modern shopper values a good deal, this is obviously a canny move by retailers who have developed a whole range of tactics to make us feel great about parting with our cash. After all, as the thinking goes, if one store can persuade the consumer that they offer the lowest prices and the best promotions, they will attract a greater number of customers. In the highly competitive world of retailing, this is highly important because as we have seen throughout this book, only the strongest survive.

But, when you strip away all the glitz, gloss and colour, how much of a bargain are we really getting? How many of these great, unmissable, deals are actually genuine price reductions?

The answer is: Not as much as we'd all like to think.

In truth, many of these offers are not so special after all. Indeed, according to one survey of more than 700,000 grocery products sold in our major grocers over the period of a year, there are dodgy deals on everything from fresh fruit to pet food[78]. Time and again, supermarkets manipulated their offers to give the illusion of great savings, when in reality there was very little, to no reductions whatsoever. In some cases, products on so-called special offer were more expensive than had been previously listed!

Misleading promotions abound, including doubling the price of single items before they went on multi-buys, so the item would cost more per item on the promotion than when it was bought before or after the date. Another favourite is to label a product as 'was at' a high price and 'now at' a lower one, when there is no evidence whatsoever of it ever having being sold at the higher price. Many 'offers' last throughout most of the year, even though the breathless blurb says they are ending in a week's time.

Perhaps most interestingly though, it works. According to the same research which questioned the truth behind the promotions, two-fifths of consumers admitted that these offers encouraged them to buy products they didn't really need, even though a third said they had gone on to regret their impulse purchase.

It is therefore hardly surprising that retailers have become increasingly inventive over the years with their special offers despite the successive efforts from the government to crack down on misleading pricing with legislation ranging from the Consumer Protection Act of 1987, to the most recent Consumer Protection from Unfair Trading Regulations Act of 2008. The current rules make it an offence for traders to treat consumers unfairly through misleading actions, misleading omissions or aggressive practices. But, has that changed anything? Not a bit of it.

The rule which has been most open to abuse is the '28-day rule' which says that the 'was' price, i.e. the price before discount, must have been on offer for at least 28 days before the special offer. The product also shouldn't be on offer for longer than it was on sale at the original higher price and retailers shouldn't refer to a price which was available more than six months ago.

[78] Which? June 2012 Supermarket special offers exposed

Although the 28-day rule sounds great in theory, retailers have been highly inventive in the ways they have learned to work around it.

The most vulnerable part of the ruling is that the 28 days do not necessarily have to apply to the particular store which is promoting the special offer. Thus, if you had a huge retail chain selling, let's say, canned tuna, it could sell them at a remote branch for higher than the list price for the requisite 28 days. Then, once that period was up, the tuna could be offered at a massive '30 per cent discount' across every store in the retailer's chain. Except, thanks to the clever manoeuvring of the retailer, the can of tuna is probably simply on sale at, or at least close to, the original price.

There are a number of variations on this theme too – just to keep things interesting. After all, an ever-changing variety of promotions is just as important when giving the impression of special, special offers.

Imagine, for example, that our retailer wants to make an offer for household candles a BOGOF. BOGOF is the retail term for a Buy One, Get One Free promotion and this has long been a highly popular element of the retail special offer armoury.

Let's say that the list price for this box of scented candles is £1.50. What our canny retailer will most likely do is put it on sale in the remote branch for £2.80 for the requisite 28 days, while continuing to sell it everywhere else at the usual £1.50. Then, at the right moment, it will create a nationwide special offer which says: Scented candles £2.80 - Buy One, Get One Free. The apparently incredible offer will be promoted with huge banners and all the bells and whistles the chain can throw at it.

Fantastic, the consumer will think when they can't fail but be drawn to this extraordinary offer. If they spend £2.80, they will get two boxes of scented candles, which are worth the equivalent of £5.60! What a bargain. Except it isn't. In reality, for their £2.80, they are only getting products that are worth £3 if they had bought them at that very same store only five weeks before. The fact is, it isn't anything like the good deal it is proclaiming itself to be.

There are all sorts of inventive ways to convince consumers they are getting more than they really are and the fact that the 28-day rule does not cover fruit and veg has allowed supermarkets to flex their creativity still further in the area of fresh produce. Fruit and veg are exempt from the 28-day rule because they are perishable items with a short shelf life. The thinking goes that it is not feasible for them to be on sale for nearly a month at one price before a discount was introduced, because the produce would no longer be fresh.

As a result of this anomaly, fresh produce has become a real focus for price promotions in recent times. Supermarkets compete aggressively to be ever more eye-catching and innovative in their offers and it is hardly surprising that the smaller independents don't get a look in. The style of promotions even has trends, with each decade showcasing a new and more ambitious style of offer, just to keep things fresh and interesting. Thus, the nineties were all about BOGOFs, while the turn of the millennium marked the introduction of Threefers or Twofers (Three/two products for the price of two/one). Technology has enabled retailers to become increasingly ambitious in their offers and the switch to electronic scanning at checkouts offers retailers the opportunity to create bundled deals. So, for example, if a customer buys a sandwich, a cold drink and a bar of chocolate together, with the combined price of the component parts being £5.54, the store could offer them as a £4.99 'meal deal'. The component parts don't even have to go through the till at the same time because it all gets picked up by the computer.

Yet, even though the style of promotion changes, it never seems to move towards being a better deal for the consumer. Take threefers and twofers, the post-millennium favourites. They have proved to be just as much of a minefield for the consumer as their predecessor the BOGOF. With this type of promotion its easy to end up paying a high price for less food, which is of course something the retailer fully expects to happen and even factors into their marketing budgets when they are putting together the offer.

The retailers are not doing anything illegal or underhand. The chains will mark-up their packs with clear labels showing that if you buy two packets of, say, peas, then the price is £3. Yet, somehow, many shoppers manage to miss this and only put one pack in their trolley.

Cashiers at the till rarely point out the missed promotion, which means the poor consumer will pay £2 for their single pack of peas, when they could have had double the amount for just 50 per cent more. (There is also the issue that even if they do take advantage of the twofers, many people don't get around to eating the mountain of extra fruit and veg they've bought and end up throwing it in the bin. We will, however, come to the ethics of modern retailing in the next chapter.)

The latest trend in the quest for 'great deals' is the move towards round pounds, which is, as it happens not that good a deal at all.

"Only £3!" a distinctive red sticker will scream.

Back when I was a lad, it was far more common to price up items to the nearest 99p. Marking a product as something pounds and 99p was the accepted shorthand to mean 'good value'. Thus, our £3 bargain was more likely £2.99 in 'old' money. However, thanks to the rise and rise of pound shops, mainstream stores have cottoned on to the fact that consumers see value in a different way. The 99p has been gradually dropped and replaced by round pounds. According to reports, some 16 per cent of items sold in Tesco, Asda and Sainsbury's are now priced at either £1 or £2.[79] That's not a big deal, you may think, it is only a penny more than the 99p or £1.99 they used to be, but of course those pennies all add up when you are talking about millions of transactions.

I know from my long experience in this industry that retailers spend an inordinate amount of time and manpower setting up and carefully crafting these offers. And, although they sometimes sail close to the wind, they do everything possible to keep within the letter of the law. Key to it all is the cooperation and approval of local authority trading standards officials. Trading standards offices around the country are the official enforcer of legislation to do with commercial organisations in areas from health and safety to price and keep an eye on promotions to make sure they meet the rules.

---

[79] Pound shop revolution hits the big supermarkets; The Telegraph, June 5 2012

Retail chains are at great pains to cultivate what are known as 'home authority agreements', which basically means a close relationship with the trading standards office which is geographically closest to the chain's head office. All price reductions are passed by these local officers, to see if they meet the various rules and if any trading standards officers elsewhere in the country have an issue with the actions of one chain, they defer to the home authority to decide if there has been any breach of the regulations.

This is, of course, all legal and above board and although trading standards clearly don't have the resources to check and monitor every single price, they are doing their job to the letter. Similarly, supermarkets are open with their home authorities and verify all promotions as required.

Yet, looking at the scope of the checks and balances, and knowing how 'flexible' some of these offers can be, you would be forgiven for thinking the facilities to monitor them does not quite go far enough. Similarly, although everyone keeps within the letter of the law, perhaps there is a case for discussing whether the rules are adequate for the job.

Although what we buy and where we buy it is all a matter of personal choice, the inescapable fact is, many of these promotional techniques listed here are not in the best interests of every consumer. This doesn't just mean that they may end up paying more either. Often it encourages consumers to buy things they don't need and cannot afford.

To me, the most glaring example of this is the rather enticing 'buy now, pay later' deals on home furnishings, most notably sofas. The accepted industry model is that you can walk into a store, choose a sofa and then not have to pay for it for one, two, even four years. Even if you say, no thank you, I'd like to pay for it in full now and can I have a discount, they won't. Why? Because this is how the model works and the credit would not be interest-free if you could get a discount to pay upfront.

To explain this in more detail, let's first dissect who makes what out of the transaction. Imagine a sofa that is on sale at a large retailer for £2,000. The marketing at this major chain says that you can have this fabulous model for £2,000, and don't have to pay a penny for a year and then get three extra years credit interest-free. Built in within that cost is the payment for the actual sofa and the charge for the credit. The debt is then sold on to a financial services provider, which will own the debt for four years and will collect the payment from the consumer.

In the majority of cases, there is no way to simply pay the price of the sofa upfront and get the interest charge removed from the sale to buy it at, say, £1,500 because the credit would not be interest-free. The only way the sofa companies can be assured of an acceptable volume of mass sales is to stick to the interest-free model which has been agreed by trading standards officials and stick to it rigidly they do.

Of course, what seems like such a good offer at the time can turn out to be a bit of a headache for some consumers, particularly when the economy takes a downturn. Faced with a choice of paying off the sofa or putting food on the table, some families will struggle. The reality of living beyond their means will hit and for some the end of the interest-free period will be a dreadful moment. Hence the financial services companies which work with the sofa companies must factor into their calculations the possibility that some buyers will default, or others will not have the required money and will want to pay it off in instalments with interest.

None of this is to say that retailers shouldn't offer interest-free financing, but there is a moral argument that such promotions are not always in the best interest of consumers. In among the noise of such enticing promotions, it is not always easy to check yourself and remember that retailers are out there to make money. Faced with a fantastic offer, it is hard to remind yourself that the companies that set them up have developed their ideas after extensive study of the psychology of human beings. They know exactly what buttons to push to get us to purchase pretty much anything.

In a lot of cases, retailers are helped by the fact that no one does really question the facts behind promotions. Indeed, if you asked most people, they probably won't remember the terms which prompted them to grab one special offer or another in the first place. Indeed, when I talked earlier in this book about the miraculous changes bestowed onto the retail environment by the advent of the humble barcode, I did not mention one other amazing bonus from these innocuous-looking little strips of black and white:

No one has a clue about the price they pay for their goods any more.

In the old days, each product was painstakingly priced-up by hand. I can still vividly remember as a young shop assistant the pride I used to take over the speed I could mark-up an entire palate of produce with a hand-held pricer, brushing it past each pack or tin at the rate of knots and leaving behind a small sticky label declaring its value.

Today though, each product you buy is a blank sheet price-wise. Sure, when you see it on the shelf there will be a label showing its cost, which is even broken down to price per kilogram, but once you have dropped it into your basket or trolley, that is the last you will see of those numbers. When you get it home and put it in the fridge, larder or cupboard, you will have no idea what you paid, unless you work through a list of numbers on your receipt.

Although it has become a staple joke that no one knows the price of a pint of milk anymore, not even our own Prime Minister and Chancellor of the Exchequer, who have been dismissed as 'two posh boys who don't know the price of milk'[80], who can really blame us. It is not information that is readily available to hand, so why would we know?

Of course, if there was a price label, you would probably be more likely to scrutinise things more regularly, perhaps when you are loading them into your store cupboard. You'd maybe notice that the price of a tin of soup had gone up from £1 to £1.25, before being reduced 'on offer' to 99p, but today that just isn't likely to happen. For the time-poor consumer, who probably has other things to worry about than the price of individual groceries, the helpful clues are no longer there.

[80] BBC News – Should politicians know the price of a pint of milk, 24 April 2012

Retailers know we can't recall the prices we are paying and can play any game they like with their promotions in the safe knowledge that no one is likely to notice. Even if they do get rumbled, they can put up the "we're only human, sometimes we make mistakes" defence which they used in reply to the Which? expose of bogus special offers.[81]

To make things even worse, we the consumer are even complicit in some of the nonsense around price promotions. For some inexplicable reason, we have become so wedded to the promotional noise all around us that we will cling on to it come what may.

Take, as an example, the sale of new kitchens. It doesn't matter if you buy them from B&Q, or Wickes or Homebase, virtually no kitchens are sold at full price. Everyone waits patiently for the January, Easter or Autumn sales so they can buy their new units at 50 per cent off. No one would even consider buying them at any other time.

So, the retailer has pretty much the rest of the year to establish a 'full price', according to the 28-day rule and then in the magical months of January, April and October can, like a magician pulling a rabbit from a hat, slash the price in two.

It doesn't take a genius to work out that the 'full price' that has been diligently established is actually double the retail value of the kitchen, allowing the store to halve its price with no pain to its profit margin whatsoever. The retailer is happy because they are selling their kitchens and the consumer is delighted with their bargain.

As I discovered when I joined Wickes, it is virtually impossible to break this pattern. I had always thought that this practice was outdated and faintly ludicrous and leading a company which operated this system only served to reinforce this view. Apart from anything else, it was seriously disruptive to the business. We'd have to gear up for a massive peak in kitchen sales concentrated over a one-month period, bringing in extra staff and equipment. It was chaotic and disruptive to the rest of the business. For a retailer, a system like this is the worst possible scenario.

[81] Which? June 2012 Supermarket special offers exposed

Gathering together the Wickes team, I posed what was to me a blindingly obvious question. Wouldn't it be a lot simpler to stop marking up a £500 kitchen to £1,000 during the year before discounting it and selling it at £500 in the sales months, and simply sell it at the lower price all the year around? That way we wouldn't have to cope with peaks in demand. Surely the practice known in the retail trade as 'every day low pricing' (EDLP) could work in kitchen sales? It might even given Wickes a new USP (unique selling proposition). Come to Wickes for a cut-price kitchen *all year round*.

Try as I might though, no one was interested. Even my own team made it perfectly clear that they thought it would never work. They were convinced that the public would never respond positively to such a stance. So, even today, most people patiently wait until the sale months to buy something they could have had at any month in the year if they were not indoctrinated by the fact that you are 'daft' unless you buy these big ticket items in the sales.

Another perfect example of how willing we all are to dance to the tune of major retailers is the explosive growth in loyalty cards. As a nation, we Britons love loyalty schemes. From Green Shield stamps in the sixties and seventies, to the more modern plastic credit card style schemes, we've all collected points with gusto. In fact, since Tesco first introduced their Clubcard in 1995, offering regular shoppers vouchers giving discounts, loyalty schemes have multiplied at an alarming rate. More than 15 million people now have a Tesco Clubcard. Retailers from Boots, to WHSmith to petrol stations have got in on the act and about 85 per cent of households have at least one loyalty card[82]. Many people have wallets or purses stuffed full of the things.

Yet, while shoppers undoubtedly benefit from discounts thanks to the cards, there is another side to these schemes. Firstly, loyalty schemes, like so many retail promotions, offer very little, if any, value to the consumer because it can take a considerable amount of shopping before any meaningful discount is forthcoming. At Tesco, for example, consumers are rewarded with a point worth a penny for every pound spent. Boots gives a more generous rate of four points, worth 4p in the

[82] TNS

pound, but even then shoppers would have to spend a fair bit before getting a great deal back.

What should be perhaps of more concern, is the fact that stores are obtaining vast amounts of detailed personal information about their customers and their habits in return for these schemes. The question we should be asking is; are we selling our personal information at a realistic price?

The moment your loyalty card is swiped at the till, it adds a list of everything you've just bought to an electronic database. This database enables individual retailers to quietly build a profile about you, mapping your shopping preferences, travel habits and even how environmentally friendly you are. The end result is a massive pool of consumer data which can be used to paint a complete picture of our lives, classifying our wealth, lifestyles and even personality traits such as whether we are adventurous or conservative. In the early days, this data was sold by the retailer to manufacturers and marketing agencies for considerable sums of money.

In the days before their introduction, retailers vied for our attention with indiscriminate advertising, mass marketing and offers, hoping that some of this would stick. However, now they know more about shoppers as individuals, rather than as a generic mass, they can be far more manipulative. Knowledge is, after all, power.

Early on in the loyalty card boom, US grocery giant Walmart was reported to have used data from its loyalty scheme to spot a trend for fathers to come into its stores on the way home from work on a Friday and buy nappies. The store placed a (slightly incongruous) display of six packs of beer beside the baby goods and sales went up.

Since then, retailers and in particularly supermarkets, have been increasingly savvy in the way they use their loyalty card data. Pundits are already predicting that the information will be used in all sorts of new areas, including personal finance, which is a sector on the radar of most major chains, with many already offering basic services.

And what a great position they will be in to expand into personal finance. Today, when consumers fill in an application form for motor insurance, the insurer only asks keys facts such as age, driving history, occupation, postcode and the make of car. At a stroke, the applicant is lumped in with all the other people who fit largely the same profile and the same rate will apply to all.

If the insurer knew more about you, it might be able to fine-tune the premiums to more accurately reflect the risk. And, who is in a perfect place to do just this? Yes, supermarkets which have been logging your every move for years. They'll know before anyone has even signed the application that a 20-a-day smoker, who buys upwards of 30 cans of beer a week, is a worse insurance risk. Plus, they'll be able to target shoppers more effectively too. A regular buyer of pet food is an obvious candidate for a pet insurance mailer, for example.

The irony of all of this is, having opened up our heart and soul and given up every piece of personal information imaginable in exchange for a few pennies off, many people don't even spend their loyalty points. According to research[83], British shoppers are sitting on £5.2 billion of unused loyalty card points, with 36 per cent of consumers not knowing what their points were worth, or what rewards they could be converted into. Yet, although 18 per cent admitted to having old loyalty cards which they started using but stopped, because they didn't know what they were doing, 68 per cent of those asked thought loyalty cards were 'value for money'! In a separate survey, the chemist and cosmetics company Boots says that over 1,000 customers are sitting on over £260 benefits which they have not spent, while a third of its customers have more than £5 sitting around unspent.

So, we are in a situation where most people don't take advantage of their loyalty cards, but for those that do the rewards are pitiful and the bulk of the advantage is down to retailers who reap the rewards of a rich database of knowledge.

Yet again, the consumer is the loser.

---

[83] £5.2bn in loyalty card points going begging in Britain, Daily Mail, 1 June 2010

At least part of the reason we have got to this state of affairs is that consumers have, quite simply, lost all their bargaining power. In years gone by trading was all about a two-way conversation between the seller and the buyer. Shoppers like my mother Louie would trawl shops up and down the High Street where they had a direct relationship with the men and women who ran the shops. They got to know each other, their likes, dislikes and preferences, and this was the source of a great deal of good-hearted banter. In my mother's case, for example, Winkle Lamb, the fishmonger, knew Louie was partial to herrings, and would let her know when a good fresh catch was on its way. Similarly, Freestones the bakers would always tip her the wink as to which was the freshest baked bread of all the ones on display.

On the market stalls, which I have mentioned so many times in this book, there was a direct relationship with the shopper too, even though there was a higher rate of passing trade. Here the communication was all based on noise. Standing beside the bright, neatly laid-out produce, littered with large pricing signs marked up in the sweeping strokes of a black marker pen, would be the larger-than-life presence of the stallholder.

"Every bowl of fruit a pound," they'd be yelling. "Snow white cauliflowers, come on girls, come on girls."

And there was a rapport too. Even though we had already lost our ability to barter in the same way as they still do in many of the Eastern country markets, back then, no self-respecting shopper would have just handed over their pound for a bowl of apples. No, they'd have launched into a good bit of banter and maybe the price was bartered to 90p. It may sound like I am looking back on the time with rose tinted spectacles, but as anyone who lived through that era will attest, shopping was a lot more fun in those days.

Many people will be familiar with the thrill of bartering in foreign markets on holiday, but why can't we do it back home today? Nowadays, no one really barters anymore. All of that interaction has been drilled out of society by the rush towards automation and economies of scale. Now that shopping is pretty much a self-service activity, no one needs to talk to one another any more.

This left large retailers with a bit of a conundrum. How do you sell to people in the modern world? After all, if there is minimal interaction, there is nothing to stop a consumer shopping elsewhere. There is no loyalty and the retailer has no real platform to negotiate (or at least seem to be negotiating).

The solution that rapidly spread across large shop chains became an industry all of its own: Point of Sale (POS) material. Shelf wobblers, giant posters, leaflet holders and banners proliferated and became the way that shops now communicate. And, if you are going to communicate via the printed page, the best way to differentiate yourself from your rivals is to offer something cheaper.

Shoppers are faced with a wealth of colourful POS, enticing them to buy this, that or the other and invariably they boast of the most incredible offers. Each BOGOF or Twofer is designed to seem better than the next in order to attract our attention.

The POS is the noise of the modern retail environment. Sadly though, unlike the market stall environment of old, it is a one-way interaction. In fact, the only bargaining power the consumer now has is choosing where they want to shop and which brands they buy once they are there, because they no longer have the platform to negotiate. This state of affairs makes shoppers vulnerable to promotional stories which are not as real as they first look.

The corollary of this is that the more consumers see their power diminished, the more power is wielded by large retailers.

However, it is not all doom and gloom. There is a glimmer of change on the horizon. There are signs that consumers are starting to get irritated and turned off by promotions in these days of double dip recession and austerity. The fact that discounters such as Aldi, and Lidl, as well as pound shops, are seeing exponential, double-digit, growth, says to me that shoppers are voting with their feet. These stores don't generally dabble in glitzy promotions, sticking to the more simple, yet clearly effective, EDLP model. Their growing popularity is delivering a clear message that EDLP is what consumers want, not a bunch of fancy promotions which no one really understands and which just don't seem to add up. People who have less money in their purses, want to know that they are getting good value and many are canny enough to know that not all large retailers have their best interest at heart.

The fact is, retailers don't need to rely so heavily on these essentially meaningless marketing and promotion gimmicks. Indeed, if we look back at retail history, there is a compelling precedent of how one retailer ditched them altogether and thrived. I mentioned in chapter one how Tesco boldly dropped Green Shield stamps in 1977 in the face of mounting inflation that was making promotions more meaningless than they already were. The replacement, Checkout 77, was based on EDLP throughout the whole store after the money that was spent on the stamp promotion was channelled into a TV campaign to inform customers of their initiative and a dramatic cut in prices. As a result, Tesco's market share went from seven per cent to virtually 14 per cent overnight.

Arguably, the current economic squeeze is like 1977 all over again. We are not blighted by rampant inflation, but austerity and lack of money are having an impact all around. The question is, will major retailers note the signals and break their attachment to promotional deals? Or will they experience resistance just as I discovered at Wickes when I tried to drop the reliance on January sales?

Perhaps this time it is up to consumers to vote with their wallets, as so many are already beginning to do. However, until there is any noticeable change, all consumers would do well to remember the old adage: there is no such thing as a free lunch.

Chapter Nine
Ethical and environmental trading –
What price guilt free shopping?

It takes two to tango. There is no point waiting for retailers to save the world. Consumers need to join in too.

I can still remember the great plastic bag debate as clearly as though it happened yesterday. Seated alongside a dozen or more senior colleagues around the large boardroom table in Tesco's Cheshunt headquarters, the subject which was getting everyone hot under the collar was; should we give away free plastic bags to shoppers?

The year was 1987, and plastic bags had been available at our checkouts for around a decade. Customers either used them, or one of the large supplies of cardboard boxes which were stacked up at the front of the store in the so-called cardboard box corral. Those bags and boxes had been the next stage in evolution from the elasticated string bags my mother Louie used to religiously take with her every time she went to the High Street.

Until then though, the only type of plastic carrier bag in circulation was made out of low-density polyethylene, which is a good, strong, tear-resistant plastic. You'd recognise the type of thing today as the colourful, branded, bags given out by fashion stores. Customers immediately took to the low-density polyethylene bags, but they were expensive to manufacture and supply, so Tesco had always charged shoppers a few pence per bag. Most people re-used the strong bags, thanks to the charge and also because the habit of grabbing a re-useable bag before every shop was still deeply ingrained in the psyche of most households, thanks to the humble string bag.

Then, high-density polyethylene bags were invented. The plastic in these bags is thinner and gives that characteristic crackly and crinkly sound when crushed. Bags made from high-density polyethylene are not as tear-resistant as their low-density cousins, but, importantly, they cost a fraction of the amount to make.

So, should we give them away free as a marketing gimmick?

"It would make sense in terms of good customer service," I said, opening the debate in my role as Tesco's then customer services director. "The cost to us would be nominal."

Dennis Tuffin, Tesco's retail operations director, was characteristically forthright.

"I'll tell you what good customer service is, shall I?" he scoffed, looking me straight in the eye with a challenging stare. "Let's not just stop at giving customers free carrier bags and packing the things for them at the checkout. Why don't we take the groceries home for them, or cook them, or hell, let's give them the whole damn lot for free!"

Although Tuffin was being typically combative, it was hard not to concede that he did have a point. After all, Tesco was then and indeed still is a commercial organisation and as such is there to make money. Yes, it wants to provide excellent customer service and make the whole shopping experience as convenient as possible, but it can never lose sight of the fact that it has to be at a profit. We had to weigh up the potential that shoppers may be inclined to spend more if they had access to a plentiful supply of free carrier bags, versus the cost to Tesco of supplying millions of bags to give away every year.

The debate raged back and forth that day, but with the precedent that other retailers around the world were beginning to offer free bags at the checkout, our hand was to some extent forced. We were acutely aware that it was something our customers would soon come to expect and if we didn't meet those expectations they could easily go elsewhere to spend their money. So, the decision was made. Tesco, like almost every single other retailer here and around the world, started offering free, single use, bags at the checkout.

Fast forward to today and the impact of that decision, and others like it from rival retailers, is plain to see. Every year 800,000 tonnes of single use plastic bags are given out in the European Union, with the UK accounting for 6.75 billion[84] individual bags picked up at the checkout.

---

[84] Waste and Resources Action Programme (WRAP)

On average, shoppers use 8.6 single use bags a month, yet just six per cent of them get recycled.

Environmental campaigners estimate that the bags, which only get used for an average of twenty minutes, when we load them up with our groceries and then take them home and unpack them, then take up to 1,000 years to degrade after we discard them. Like all forms of plastic, they don't biodegrade completely either, they photodegrade, breaking up into smaller and smaller toxic bits that contaminate the soil and waterways.

Many bags don't make it to landfill. They end up as waste on our beaches, streets and parks and become an environmental eyesore. They can cause serious harm to birds or marine animals, which mistake them for food and swallow them, with painful and often fatal consequences.

The plastic bag issue has been on the international radar for a while now and governments around the world have had a go at tackling it in a variety of different ways, with various degrees of success. A number of countries have instigated a ban on high-density plastic bags, including China, South Africa, Taiwan and Bangladesh. Indeed, Bangladesh was one of the first countries to ban them after major and catastrophic flooding there caused by plastic bag litter blocking drains. A handful of countries, such as Rwanda and Somalia, have gone one step further and banned plastic bags altogether.

In Europe, the response has been more fragmented. Italy became the first country in the EU to ban non-biodegradable plastic bags in 2011, after first experimenting with a tax on carrier bags, which had little impact. Other countries, such as Denmark and Germany, have established taxes, or recycling fees, on the use of their plastic bags, while in Paris, the use of non-biodegradable plastic bags has been banned in large stores since 2007.

Meanwhile, in the UK, early attempts to tackle the problem were on a purely voluntary basis. In 2008, the UK Government made an agreement with retailers to encourage customers to cut down on the number of single use bags used by 50 per cent. Although the numbers of bags used did fall dramatically, it fell short of targets and in fact, in recent years, usage has started to creep back up. Indeed, in 2011/12, the use of carrier bags rose by 5.4 per cent, continuing the pattern of a steady rise after a brief four years of decline.[85]

Today, the situation is more fragmented and confused than ever with Wales operating a levy of 5p per bag, Scotland in consultation about a 'bag tax' and in Northern Ireland, bags will cost 5p from April 2013. Some districts in England have organised localised voluntary bag bans, most notably Modbury in south Devon, where campaigner Rebecca Hosking, a BBC camera woman, persuaded 34 local shops to substitute their plastic bags with reusable cloth bags after she was moved by witnessing turtles and dolphins choking to death on plastic while filming in the Pacific. Prime Minister David Cameron has issued a veiled threat that unless retailers in England drastically reduce bag usage they will be forced to by law, but as yet there are no real signs of action.

In all the undercurrent of protest against the ubiquitous single use bag, the focus is predominantly on the government and retailers. The Daily Mail which has been running a long-running Banish the Bags campaign, which kicked off with a dramatic nine page spread in February 2008 graphically depicting the environmental impact of plastic waste, wants the government to force retailers to reduce the amount they hand out to customers. While Friends of the Earth advises consumers to get into the habit of carrying around reusable bags, it doesn't pull any punches with its calls on the government and retailers to do their bit to reduce plastic waste.

It could be argued though, the emphasis is all wrong. Going back to my plastic bag debate at Tesco, at the core of everything is the fact that supermarkets are commercial operations. They are there to make a profit. To expect a major retailer to voluntarily sacrifice some of its bottom line in favour of good causes, is all very nice, but how realistic an expectation is it? Apart from anything else, in the highly competitive world of retail, no store group wants to break ranks and take away something customers essentially like. They know it would be commercial suicide because shoppers will simply go elsewhere to stores which offer them what they want.

[85] Waste and Resources Action Programme (WRAP)

To me, there are two obvious options here. The first is for the government to impose a compulsory plastic bag tax, to force all the retailers to act. However, the *full charge* for the bag should go to green causes, but more of that in a moment.

The second, is for the consumer to stop waiting for everyone to tell them what to do and make a stand for themselves.

It may be an unpopular question to pose (and the fact that it comes from a retailer won't make it any easier for some people to stomach) but here goes: isn't it about time that consumers shouldered some of the blame for the damage we all do to our green and pleasant land?

Although there are dozens of campaign groups trying to stop general usage of plastic bags and the 'bag for life' campaign has gained a large and loyal following, the fact remains that it is all too easy for the population as a whole to carry on regardless. Consumers can point the finger firmly at the authorities, or at retailers, for making it too easy for them to slip their shopping into a single use bag. Then they can sleep easy at night, knowing it is someone else's fault.

Well, as I often used to say to my store teams when they were complaining about others; don't be too quick to point the finger because when you do, there are always three fingers pointing back at you.

We, the consumer, should take considerably more responsibility for the plastic bag explosion all around us. There is probably not a person in the land who hasn't taken the easy option of picking up a single use bag, at least once, rather than supplying their own means of taking their shopping home. Often, we don't even think twice about it. I freely admit that I have resorted to using the free bags many times myself, despite having a cupboard full of plastic bags, and bags for life, at home. After all, it is a lot easier to pick up a single use carrier bag at the checkout, rather than going to the trouble of remembering to take your own, so why not?

The apparently guilt-free, ongoing, use of plastic bags is just another symptom of the consumer's almost complete disregard for the long-term implications of their shopping experience. In the pell-mell rush towards lower prices and convenience, hardly anyone gives a second thought to what it all means to the planet. And why not? After all, we are the baby boomer generation that grew up wanting everything when it was short. We developed and instilled into our children a 'you can have everything' culture. This greed has become endemic.

This laissez faire attitude pervades every aspect of retailing, not just grocery shopping and when it comes to discussing ethics and the High Street, plastic bag use is not the only sector of the market that should be put under the microscope. Fast fashion, a clothing trend which sees t-shirts sold for as little as a pound, cannot go unexamined in this context because it is yet another questionable practice we have readily embraced, with little thought to the long-term, or even short-term, consequences.

The fast fashion trend really took off in the 1990s, when clothing brands were looking for new ways to increase profits. Many traditional clothing chains were spooked by the fact that supermarkets were developing their own, low cost, lines at the time and recognised they needed a new, reliable revenue stream, and fast. Although the grocers' flirtation with fashion only started with simple t-shirts, jeans and underwear, it was obvious to everyone it was not going to stop there. Sure enough, when fashion guru George Davies moved from Next to Asda, it signalled a new era for supermarket clothing and the search for the next big thing took on a new sense of urgency.

The first port of call for many fashion companies was to re-examine their supply chains and luckily for them, globalisation paved the way for them to shift the bulk of their production to the developing world. With labour and overheads at a fraction of the cost of those closer to home, clothing brands were able to produce more collections per year, at a lower cost. Fast fashion was born and consumers could not get enough of it.

As clothing brands became more comfortable with worldwide commerce, they began to split manufacturing capabilities. Thus, standard lines, with long lead times could be made abroad for a fraction of the cost, to keep the stores well stocked with super-cheap t-shirts, jeans and shoes. Plus, factories were deployed closer to home so a hot new look, seen on the celebrity of the moment, could be copied, manufactured and put on the clothes rails at a store near you within days. As a way to keep fashion stores looking bang on trend, all the time, and stuffed full of hundreds of different up-to-the-minute styles, it was a winner.

Customers loved this speeding up of fashion and the fact that everything has become so affordable means a garment can be bought, worn and discarded within days. It doesn't matter if you are rich or poor either. It is now acceptable across the entire social spectrum to spend less than the cost of a light lunch on an entire outfit from a value retailer. Indeed, consumers now buy 40 per cent of their clothes at value retailers, with just 17 per cent of their clothing budget.[86] The market for low cost clothing, espoused by clothing giants Primark and TK Maxx as well as the major supermarket chains, has increased 45 per cent over the past five years to more than £6 billion. It seems no one is immune to the lure of fast fashion and there are few people around who won't admit to the thrill of buying a nice outfit for less than the cost of a takeaway.

Yet, just as with the plastic bags there is a wider, environmental cost. We discard two million tonnes of clothes a year[87] and the bulk of it is simply tossed into landfill. It is estimated that the UK clothing sector produces 3.1m tonnes of carbon dioxide, 2m tonnes of waste and 70m tonnes of waste water every year.

Indeed, a House of Lords committee waste reduction report in 2008, observed that the culture of fast fashion encourages consumers to; "dispose of clothes which have only been worn a few times in favour of new, cheap garments which themselves go out of fashion and be discarded within a matter of months."

Of course, fast does not mean free. When the cost of goods decreases at such a rate, someone, somewhere is paying. It could be a poorly remunerated factory worker in the Far East who works in less than ideal conditions while being put under pressure to meet ever-shorter deadlines. Or, closer to home there is the three tons of damaging

---

[86] TNS Worldpanel (2006) Fashion Focus
[87] DEFRA

carbon dioxide emissions each year from the discarded clothes.[88] This is not to mention the cost of the cheap fibres that make up the clothes we buy for next to nothing. Both polyester and cotton, which together account for more than 80 per cent of fibre production worldwide, present issues when it comes to sustainability. Man-made polyester is petroleum-based and supplies of petrol are dwindling, whereas growing cotton requires vast amounts of the most precious resource on Earth, water.

All of this comes before you get to the environmental cost of transporting all these goods halfway around the world into the (plastic) bags of the eager shopping public.

Of course, when it comes to the environmental impact of transportation of goods over large distances, it's not just fashion. When we are talking about indulging our every whim, whatever the cost, there is also the question of our year-round appetite for food from around the world, such as Kenyan fine beans and strawberries from Saudi Arabia. UK food imports grew by 51 per cent between 1990 and 2005 and with a corresponding decrease in domestic agricultural output, there is a growing dependence on these goods from abroad.[89]

Fair enough, you may say, the consumer has not covered themselves in glory. But, surely retailers do have a case to answer and should set an example by behaving more responsibly. Shoppers are, after all, only buying what has been put in front of them. However, what we must constantly remind ourselves, is that retailers are commercial organisations in a highly competitive sector. Although store chains want to be seen as the good guys, it is very rare to non-existent that they will put themselves to any sort of commercial disadvantage just to gain a bit of kudos.

The people at the top of these retail organisations see it as their job to compete and provide the consumer with the best possible value so they keep coming back again and again. The retail bosses are acutely aware that for the majority of consumers these days, the *best value* means the *lowest prices.* Saving the planet just doesn't come into the equation when shoppers are making their choices.

---

[88] DEFRA

[89] WWF – Environmental impacts of the UK food economy

Being environmentally friendly or super ethical, is just not number one in their business plan. Apart from anything else, it is impossible to be environmentally responsible and greedy for growth at the same time. The opening of enormous hypermarkets with acres of free parking and constant exhortations to increase consumption, frankly spells a bit of a conflict of interest. The best most chains can possibly do is to, well, do their best while *appearing* to be doing even better.

To be brutally honest; you just can't trust them.

Let's take, as an example, Marks & Spencer's much vaunted plastic bag initiative. In May 2008, M&S began charging 5p for all single use food carrier bags given out in its UK stores. The breathless press release which accompanied the announcement talked about the initiative being a 'major step towards M&S's Plan A commitments to aim to reduce carrier bag usage by a third and send no waste to landfill from its operations by 2012'.[90]

It is all laudable stuff, and the then-chief executive, Sir Stuart Rose, said that the chain's trials had already shown that charging for bags stopped around 70 per cent of customers from picking up single use bags.

The key part of the announcement though, was that all *profits* from the 5p charge, would be invested in the environmental charities such as Groundwork which will in turn invest the cash into creating or improving greener living spaces.

Let's examine this in more detail.

Before this initiative, M&S was giving away the bags for nothing and therefore shouldering the cost for the entire thing. Now, however, the costs of producing and distributing the bags are paid for out of the customer's 5p, *before* the rest of the money leftover is given away to charity. Therefore, by taking an environmental and charitable stance, the retailer has, at a stroke, got rid of a cost to the business. And, even if each bag only costs the chain a penny or two to make, those pennies

---

[90] www.marksandspencer.co.uk

soon add up when you are talking about giving away millions of bags every year.

So, let's do a back-of-the-envelope calculation as to what the High Street giant gained out of the initiative. Although M&S slashed the number of bags it gives out, from 464 million a year before the introduction of a charge, to 89 million today, it is still able to give £3 million in profits to good causes. The chain says openly that the profit per bag is 1.5p, which means that it is paying its own costs of 3.5p per bag out of the 5p charge. That equates to £3.1 million in costs taken out of the business (89 million bags x 3.5p) every year, or over the four years since the initiative began, this means M&S has saved itself a tidy £12.4 million. Not a bad extra profit on the back of the PR gains out of being an ethical trader.

M&S is not alone in this. As a retailer, I have to put my hands up to the odd bit of greenwash – with the added proviso that my intentions were always good. When I was in Hong Kong, running Whampoa's Park 'n' Shop supermarket, I was very aware of the issue of plastic bag pollution. The streets were strewn with the things and they clogged up the harbour and waterways. I hated going outside and seeing the logo of my store staring up at me from one of our bags which had been discarded on the street. It didn't look good and it didn't reflect well on the chain.

We managed to source some biodegradable plastic bags and the Park 'n' Shop publicity machine made a lot of noise about our new environmental stance. It worked out really well for us, because we had first mover advantage over our competitors and everyone in the area saw us as the green supermarket chain.

But, if I am really honest, the perception was far better than the reality. Even though I do personally feel very strongly about green issues, the biodegradable bags that were on the market back then took at least 50 years to break down once they are in landfill. Plus, an essential part of this decomposition is sunlight which breaks down the starch in the plastic. If a biodegradable bag is at the bottom of a heap of a bunch of other rubbish, there is not much chance of it getting any sunlight, is there?

I'm afraid I'm not alone in this. Many retail initiatives in this area are quite similar. In a lot of cases, there is far more PR fluff, than actual value to the environment.

Some of this is to do with the structure of large retail organisations, where individuals in each department are given clear, often really tough, targets to meet. In the race to keep costs low, and margins high, often such niceties as looking after the planet, or sustainable living, are forgotten.

The affects are widespread. Indeed, just as small High Street chains have felt the cost of supermarkets' aggressive expansion, farmers and the environment have taken a hit too.

Witness the furore in the summer of 2012, when UK farmers finally declared enough is enough and widespread protests erupted against declining payments for milk. Farmers blockaded processing plants in Leeds, Shropshire and Leicestershire claiming that cuts in the price paid to suppliers, combined with rising feed costs, could force them out of business. The trigger for the protest was a proposed cut of 2p per litre in the amount they received from processors which were set to come into force in August 2012 and followed cuts earlier in the year.

At the time of writing this book, this is still an ongoing situation, but it may help to add in some background to understand where we are.

Some smaller supermarket chains have been deliberately pricing milk at, or even below, cost as a loss leader to attract footfall into their stores. This practice, although welcomed by cost conscious consumers, obviously puts pressure on to force prices down elsewhere, a downwards spiral begins and the only loser is the UK farmer.

This practice has been helped by the fact it is now possible to buy milk sourced from farms in places in Eastern Europe where costs are lower. The dairy produce can be loaded up onto containers and shipped across Europe overnight, to be bottled and placed on the shelves within a matter of hours. The large dairy companies which act as the middlemen, and process and deliver the milk, such as Robert Wiseman Dairies, Dairy Crest and Wiseman, have made cuts in the prices they pay to UK farmers, but are still unable to compete with the cheaper produce overseas.

Meanwhile many UK farmers face losing up to 5p *per litre* of milk from their cows. Annual income for the average dairy farmer has now fallen by over £66,000 since March 2012[91], threatening the viability of rural livelihoods up and down the country.

Now, no supermarket chain would like to be responsible for killing off the UK's dairy industry because no one wants that and in PR terms that is not good. However, lower down the hierarchy in the chain, there is a milk buyer with the sole responsibility to buy the liquid at the lowest possible price. They work with the dairy companies to weigh up what they can get it for close to home and also from further afield, add in the transportation costs and so on and the lowest bid gets the contract. Ideally, everyone would like to buy closer to home, but if the local farmer cannot shave their prices, it is too bad. The cold, hard, commercial fact is that it is all down to price. (And don't forget that the background to this is the constant demand from you and I, the consumer, who wants our goods at the keenest possible cost.)

None of this is to say that retailers are complete heartless machines, who don't give a damn. Many can, and do, spend an awful lot of money on environmental projects and a number of the larger supermarket chains have been working closely with farming groups for some time to ensure a fair price for dairy goods. Indeed, in 2005, when US giant Walmart announced it was going green and pledged to be a 'good steward for the environment', other chains sensed change was afoot and quickly followed announcing an incredible array of environmental initiatives. In 2006, for example, Tesco announced it was investing £100 million in its 'environment fund'. It has invested in battery-powered home delivery trucks, automated recycling machines in stores to help customers recycle waste and it has even pledged to take thousands of lorry loads off the roads by switching wine distribution to barges on Manchester's Ship Canal.

Sainsbury's, which has launched a steady range of policies in recent years and which was the first supermarket to implement a voluntary code of conduct for ethical trading, announced an all singing, all dancing sustainability plan in 2011; 2020, which promises to achieve twenty

---

[91] Dodd Accountants

ambitious goals by 2020. Asda, like many other chains, now lists carbon cutting activities in its annual report and has pledged a 20 per cent in emissions from individual stores.

Elsewhere, although M&S's plastic bag initiative appears to raise a few questions, the chain has made good inroads in other environmental and ethical policies. The chain scores highly in a table produced by pressure group Ethical Consumer[92], particularly in areas such as refrigeration for its commitment to switch all fridges to those using gases with the lowest climate impact. It also gains plaudits for it work with NGOs and its own suppliers on saving water and managing its own 'water footprint'.

The Co-op chain scores highest in this area, winning praise for animal welfare activities, largely on the back of its policy on sustainable fish sourcing, as well as for its commitment to workers' rights and ethical trading.

Yet, look more deeply at many of these initiatives and they are filled with contradictions and evasions. Take the often raised question of refrigeration in supermarkets. It seems there are a number of much-publicised ideas on how to reduce the consumption of climate changing gases called hydrofluorocarbons, but most chains are reluctant to even discuss that most basic of environmental technologies called a door. The fact remains that no shop can really call itself environmentally friendly if its fridges and freezers don't have doors, yet, chains are unwilling to take this step. Why? Because in cold, hard, commercial terms, they know that if they did shut up their produce in tightly sealed containers, you and I would probably buy less. Yes, for a population accustomed to the convenience of supermarket shopping, the idea of opening a door is apparently too arduous. Several chains, including Asda, have experimented with 'eco stores' where doors are fitted to fridges, but the idea still seems stubbornly stuck in the 'trial' phase. No one seems willing to take the final big step because they know very well they will lose business.

The trouble is, most chains know they can grab the headlines with eye-catching, but essentially trivial initiatives, from opening the odd eco

---

[92] www.ethicalconsumer.org/buyersguides/food/supermarkets.aspx

store, or new energy saving idea and that pretty much protects them from making any major changes. Sainsbury's 'kinetic road plates', which created green energy from the motion of customers cars, was a case in point. The idea of a 'people powered' store, first appeared in June 2009, when Sainsbury's installed the invention at its Gloucester Quays outlet and announced that the plates produced 30kWh of green energy every hour, which was enough to power the store's checkouts. The idea was immediately lambasted as 'greenwash' by critics who said the saving was nominal and was only distracting people from the real, serious issues.[93] This is not to say it is not worth trying these things, and Sainsbury's is better than most, but these initiatives are still a million miles away from tackling the real issues.

When push comes to shove though, there are simply other, more pressing, priorities for these major chains and not surprisingly, it's profit that matters the most. I am just as guilty of this attitude as other retail bosses. When I was leading the recovery at Wickes, BFG and Focus, I confess that I saw environmental and ethical concerns as a distraction from the main focus, which was trying to stay in business. Right then, I barely had time to catch my breath as I lurched from one crisis to another, let alone figure out how I could be kinder to the planet.

That is not to say that I am not personally concerned by what we are doing to the planet, or that I did not take full advantage of any green efficiencies which would actively save money. Rest assured that I, like all other retailers, was quick to implement any gains to be had from supply chain efficiencies and reduced waste collection bills through recycling projects. I simply had to be more sanguine about return on investment on anything more ambitious.

It didn't help that I was handed a perfect get-out-of-jail free card on a plate too. Although by my time at Focus the government had set certain environmental targets for all retail businesses to follow, we were permitted to make up any shortfall with 'environmental credits'. Of course, the inevitable happened and these environmental credits became tradable and got bought and sold on the market like derivatives. It made a complete nonsense of the whole idea. I remember thinking;

---

[93] The Guardian, June 17 2009, Talk of 'kinetic energy plates' is a total waste of energy

surely it would be a better idea to simply tax firms who don't meet the targets?

In all honesty too, the pressure from consumers to be more green, or recycling friendly, or fair trading, or socially responsible was never really there either though. Yes, it was on the agenda of one or two consumers, but as a retailer, wherever I worked, I was always acutely aware that what really made our customers tick was low, low prices.

You don't just need to take my word for it. In a survey of 5,500 households, to determine the UK shopper's favourite supermarket, the most important element in their choice was price, followed by value for money and then quality. Ethics came firmly at the bottom of the list, with just six per cent of customers picking it as the most important element.[94]

There are examples of this myopia when it comes to consumers role in ethical shopping everywhere we look. We vote with our wallets. Ethical consumerism – that is spending on green and fair trade food, clothing, household goods, energy, banking and travel – is still far from the norm. According to statistics, overall spend on ethical food accounts for just five per cent of a typical shopping basket.[95]

Indeed, even those consumers that are environmentally minded, often have an entirely schizophrenic attitude to retailing and the environment. On the one hand, campaigners rail against the global food chain that is believed to be responsible for producing one-fifth of greenhouse gas emissions. Yet, on the other they are still purchasing imported strawberries and peaches all the year round.

Although most of us play lip service to caring about the future of the planet, it seems the majority won't pay more for their goods, or sacrifice convenience and personal comfort. We all still want and expect retailers to take on the burden of finding solutions to environmental and ethical issues, conveniently forgetting that these same organisations have overriding commercial aspirations too.

---

[94] Grocer Gold Awards 2011, www.thegrocer.co.uk
[95] Cooperative Bank Ethical Purchasing Index

Of course, the most environmentally and ethical friendly thing to do would be for all of us to consume less. That option really is solely up to us though. Less is the one thing retailers cannot sell us and wouldn't do even if they could. The onus is therefore on the consumer to act.

The question is; now we know that we really do have the High Street we deserve, will shoppers act to do anything to shape the shopping experience of the future? Or will they stick rigidly to the quest for low cost goods and convenience, whatever the consequence?

If we all do this, maybe it isn't just the High Street we should be worried about. Our greed, and the fact that we are prepared to turn a blind eye to the less palatable results of it, is slowly destroying the planet. Is this the legacy you want to leave your children, or grandchildren, in exchange for a cheap t-shirt and some out-of-season strawberries, all carried home in a single use carrier bag?

PART THREE

The future role of the High Street

Chapter Ten
Retailing in the future

The pace of introduction of new technology has transformed retailing in the past 45 years and will continue to do so. It is only the most fleet of foot store groups that will survive.

I laugh now, when I look back at the presentation I did to Tesco's board back in 1987, when I was trying to get them to change their stance on customer services. Back then, there were no slick, full colour, PowerPoint slides, presented on a wafer thin laptop computer, or hand-held tablet. You know the sort of thing, where charts fade in and out, magically merging into one another while numbers appear to pop out of nowhere. No, all I had to grab the attention of Lord MacLaurin and the rest of the then-pretty sceptical Tesco board were acetate sheets placed on an overhead projector. The all-important words of this make-or-break presentation had to be rubbed down onto the sheets, letter-by-letter, using pages of Letraset transferrable lettering, which as anyone who has ever done this will attest is a messy, inaccurate and deeply unsatisfying process. A colleague using a thick black marker pen drew up the few graphs I could muster up, while the handout I left behind afterwards had to be typed separately on a golf ball typewriter.

Lucky enough then that I had a pretty persuasive argument for a change, because it was certainly not the presentation that swung it for me!

Things today would, of course, have been entirely different and just how different is utterly astonishing. It is something I have been forced to reflect upon a lot of late because after 45-plus years in the retail industry, like it or not, one earns the reputation of being a bit of an elder statesman of the sector. Inevitably, any discussion about my career, sooner or later will somehow get around to the question; so Bill, how much have things changed since you first started out?

The easiest way I could sum this up is by referring to a much-loved TV show of the early seventies called Catweazle. For the uninitiated, or those who are still a long way off the elder statesman moniker, Catweazle was an eccentric, dishevelled, yet loveable, eleventh century wizard who accidently time travels to the year 1969. The profusion of modern technology he finds in this era amazes poor Catweazle, who initially tries to blow out light bulbs as though they were candles, calls electricity 'elec trickery' and the telephone 'telling bone', believing all these strange new things to be a powerful form of magic. Catweazle is simply amazed by everything around him and struggles to get to grips with how much things have changed.

I know exactly how he feels. In the near five decades since I began as an apprentice butcher's boy, the retail environment has altered so much so as to be virtually unrecognisable and most of that is down to extraordinary advances in technology. Technology has made its mark in every nook and cranny of the business in ways I never could have imagined in those early days.

Take, for example, the way we used to price goods so the customer could weigh up what they were to pay. When I started out, we had to individually price every piece of stock with a device called a 'plonker'. A plonker was a plastic tube filled with ink, with a felt pad with the price embossed on it at one end. There was a whole tray of them and you'd have to select the one with the right price on it for the goods you were pricing up and use the plonker to stamp the side of those products. If the price changed, for whatever reason, or you made a mistake, you'd have to get out the methylated spirits to wipe off the price inked on the product and start all over again. That was the reality of how products were priced in 1968.

Over time, the plonkers were superseded by price guns, which spat out trails of 1.5cm long sticky labels onto the lids of products. For shop-workers like me, the challenge was always to see how quickly we could price up a pallet of boxes or tins. I prided myself on being able to price up a box of 24 tightly stacked tins in less than ten seconds. These tiny price labels, which would regularly fall off, or get attached to the wrong product on route to the checkout, were then replaced by the barcode, which, as detailed earlier revolutionised every aspect of retailing, from ordering, to promotions, to stock control, thanks to the miracle of data capture. The advent of the barcode made everything work more quickly and efficiently, for customers and stores alike, so no one really mourned the passing of the plonker or sticky price label.

Of course, what made all this possible was the most breathtaking advances in computer technology. Indeed, the machines we now have today, make the ones I set out with look like veritable quaint antiques. I mentioned the 'flimsy' back in chapter one, which was the way we recorded price changes in the old days. It was a sheet of paper with the products listed down one side, with the old price listed in a vertical column and new prices in a column beside it. After I painstakingly altered each price by hand, I'd have to send the sheet down to the computer department for it all to be keyed it into the database. I am not exaggerating when I say that this computer was as large as a generous, five bedroomed, house. It was absolutely massive.

Fast forward to today and everything that my old colleagues did on this beast could now be done on a device that fits into the palm of your hand. In fact, at practically every company I have worked at in the past 20 years, they have 'reclaimed' the old computer room and used the large square footage for meeting or conference rooms.

There are changes everywhere I look, with technology touching upon every aspect of retailing. When I arrived in Hong Kong in 1988 to head-up Hutchinson Whampoa's Park 'n' Shop, for example, there was system in place where individual stores all placed their delivery receipts and invoices into a bespoke yellow bag, which was collected and replaced with an empty bag three times a week. It was not unique – I had seen many similar systems back in the UK. However, by the time I had reached Hong Kong, technology had advanced enough for me to be able to instigate a programme to install branch computing which eliminated all that and consigned that laboriously slow system to history.

Email also became an option when I was in Hong Kong and I still remember declaring straight away that we were now a paperless office, even though many of my colleagues were reluctant to let go of their old methods and clung to their paper forms. To lead the way, I switched completely straight away, but if I am honest I did find it a hard habit to break after so many years relying on the humble pen and paper. After a while though, I proved that even an old traditionalist like me could change and of course, it was well worth the effort and everything worked a whole lot more smoothly.

It is hard not to agree that the relentless changes in retail technology have brought clear and noticeable advantages every time. Indeed, from a management point of view, they have transformed the workload because they have freed up so much time. Everything can be done more quickly and efficiently, which of course frees retailers to concentrate their energy on the bigger picture.

Without a doubt though, the biggest and most advantageous of these technological changes I have seen in my retail career is the advent of the Internet. The World Wide Web, as created by Tim Berners-Lee, appeared in 1990, but it wasn't until a few years later that organisations started to see the possibilities for commercial use. In 1994, at the same time as Netscape introduced SSL encryption data online, which was seen as essential to online shopping, Pizza Hut launched an online shop and banks began to experiment with putting their services on the Internet. The stage was set for the most extraordinary retail boom, which would transform the way we all shop. It seemed like the floodgates were opened and almost overnight buzzwords like e-commerce, e-retailing and e-tailing entered the lexicon.

This is not to say that there were not a few hiccups along the way. As a retailer, watching it evolve was a fascinating, and often highly frustrating, experience because seemingly overnight bricks and mortar chains were considered old hat and if you didn't have a dot-com after your name, no one in the City was interested. Yet, some of the early e-tailing attempts flew in the face of all sense and reason.

The root of the problem was investors who were carried away by the potential of the technology and wanted the next big idea, more than a solid business plan. They literally threw money at any bright-eyed boy or girl who came up with an online retail operation which sounded halfway credible. Investors were blindly grabbing every opportunity, without apparently stopping to consider how long it would take the Internet business to make any money, or indeed, if it ever would.

Hardly surprisingly, the e-tail party got stopped in its tracks pretty quickly once everyone sat up and realised what was going on. The dot-com bust of the year 2000, was a bit of a wake-up call for the industry, particularly through the high profile failures of companies such as Boo.com, the branded fashion e-tailer which burned through £100 million in two years and US online grocery store Webvan, which went from being a $1.2 billion company to nothing in the same amount of time. There were literally hundreds of smaller players that didn't make it either and a lot of money was wasted.

However, none of this is to say that there were not some truly remarkable success stories in this time too. Indeed, while a lot of cash was frittered away, there were some very shrewd investments being made at the same time. The most notable of these by far, must surely be Amazon, which has, without a doubt, changed the world of e-commerce.

There can hardly be a person on the planet who has not heard of Amazon which started off in 1994 as a humble bookseller. Today it is the world's largest online retailer, with revenues of $48 billion and a net profit of $631 million, and sells everything from electronics to fashion to food. It doesn't just stop there either. It also provides vital logistics for outside companies which want to get access to the 173 million customers who use its market place. For a fee, Amazon will simplify everything for its partner firms, including shipping, handling and payments. It is also a publisher, with its Kindle Direct Publishing platform which enables publishers to produce ebooks and has a Web Services arm, which is a cloud computing business that is the engine behind digital content companies, such as Spotify.

The success of the firm has been credited to the vision of its founder Jeff Bezos, who has an almost obsessive attention to detail which was apparently inspired by disciplines pioneered by Toyota in the 1950s. The car giant followed the kaizen concept of continuous improvement, which has been taken to mean 'lean' by those in the West. Under Bezos' interpretation, quality control, efficiency and the relentless elimination of defects, waste and costs, are prized.

Amazon is unashamedly and ruthlessly single-minded in its pursuit of growth. In 2011, for example, Amazon stirred up controversy when it launched a mobile phone price checking app. The app allowed shoppers to scan bar codes in bricks and mortar stores and compare prices directly with those on Amazon. The thinking behind it seemed to be that very often, consumers would go into stores, try out goods and then go home, fire up the computer and find a better deal from Amazon. So, why not make it easier for them to do this and, of course, buy from Amazon. To add insult to injury, while promoting the app, Amazon offered customers $5 off purchases made through the price checker.

Not surprisingly, retailers cried foul of the idea, saying Amazon's lower overheads allowed it to undercut competitors. They also said it was a clever strategy for getting consumers to help the Internet giant with gathering price data.

Critics could say that Amazon is responsible for eroding the traditional High Street. But, is this too simplistic? After all, it is consumers who are fixated on price and convenience and appreciate the retailer's good service, quick delivery and low prices who have helped Amazon build its business. The Internet retailer offered them what they wanted – and delivered. If you take the emotion out of it and look at it on a purely business basis, Amazon's popularity should really be no surprise.

It's not just Amazon either. Since the dot-com boom and bust of the early noughties, there are dozens of slickly run, efficient, Internet retailers vying for our hard-earned cash. New names such as ASOS, Play.com and Expedia have transformed the way we buy clothes, entertainment and travel online.

That is the magic of the Internet retailing boom. For the moment at least, e-commerce is a business model that can only keep on growing. In the UK, online shopping already accounts for more than £68 billion[96] and is seeing double-digit growth every year. E-tailing now accounts for 17 per cent of the total UK retail market and there are a number of drivers which will continue to fuel that growth. One such driver is the popularity of mobile commerce, which means people can shop via tablet

---

[96] IMRG Cap Gemini eRetail Sales index

computers and smart phones, and is seen to be the next stage in the Internet shopping 'revolution'. M-commerce, as it is known, is expected to surge as more and more consumers become comfortable with shopping from their phone and improvements in web browsing capabilities and mobile apps are only going to make things easier. Once again, Amazon has led the way, with a one-click checkout experience where the consumer can choose their product and pay within seconds. Those canny folk at the world's number one e-tailer know that the more steps they put between the consumer and the final transaction, the less likely they are to buy.

Another key driver in the soaring popularity of shopping online is the widespread domestic take-up of broadband, because speed does matter. Just because they don't have to trudge down to the High Street, or spend valuable minutes hunting for a parking space, does not mean that today's consumer is going to put up with any nonsense such as slow service when they are buying online. Broadband is now cheaper, faster and more accessible and in our quest, speed and convenience has enabled us all to be more demanding than ever.

The number of UK broadband subscribers hit the 20 million mark at the end of the second quarter of 2011[97]. According to one commentator, this take-up of super-fast Internet connections, points to a revolution in how we shop, on a par with the early growth of supermarkets back in the 1950s.[98] It is the final stage in a shift of power from producers to consumers, where shoppers vote with their wallets and drive retailers to compete harder, or at the very least offer customers something in addition to the lowest possible price.

It is no wonder that many bricks and mortar retailers have been throwing money at their online offerings, because those that are slow to react quickly go the way of the dinosaurs and for those that get it right, the sky is the limit. After a slow start, the online operations of Argos, Tesco, M&S, B&Q and Next have all now staked their claim to places in the UK's top ten Internet sites.[99] In July 2012, the High Street chain John Lewis said that 25 per cent of its sales are now generated online

[97]Ofcom
[98] Hamish McRae: Here comes the shopping revolution. The Independent, December 27, 2006.
[99] IMRG Hitwise Hot Shops List

and are growing at 40 per cent annually. A growth rate of 40 per cent is something bricks and mortar retailers used to only dream about.

The flip side to this success story is that as Internet shopping becomes ever more popular, there is less and less need for retailers to have an even spread of hypermarkets, enormous warehouse stores and High Street units dotted around the country. When the consumer has made it perfectly clear that they prefer online delivery to spending money on expensive petrol to drive to a store where the goods they want may be out of stock anyway, a retailer would be daft not to sit up and listen.

The retail climate has changed irrevocably and there is no going back. The days of the race for space, which saw some major chains adding thousands of square feet of new stores every year, are well and truly over. Not only that, it is inevitable that retailers will now start to rapidly reduce the number of their physical stores because they simply do not need the selling space. It is too much of a challenge to fill these buildings with enticing products which they know (and shoppers know) will sell better online.

The pace of change will vary according to sector. The most dramatic shifts have already occurred in music and film, where more than half of physical products, not including downloads, are now sold online[100]. As a result, there have been a number of high profile bricks and mortar casualties thanks to this trend, most notably Woolworths, MusicZone, Tower Records and Game Group which are but a few of the retail names in this area that have disappeared, after waking up too late to the fact that online retailers simply offered canny shoppers a better deal and delivered it in a way they demanded. Books have historically been one of the most vulnerable sectors too. Borders has already closed and the Waterstones chain has been under real pressure.

Electrical stores will be the next sector to come under the spotlight. Just over a quarter of big ticket electrical goods are now sold online, and that figure is rising. American electronics giant Best Buy pulled out of the UK in 2011, shelving its ambitious European expansion

[100] Verdict

plans which were announced just three years earlier. Best Buy had only opened just 11 of its planned 100 megastores before it pulled the plug. Meanwhile, rival chain Comet was sold for just £2 in November 2011. The dire state of the electronics market is not solely down to competition from the Internet, there are other factors too such as a drop in consumer spending, but online sales is still recognised as a hugely significant and growing factor.

Clothes sales have, until now, been more resilient. Just nine per cent of fashion sales are online[101] but that figure has seen steady growth too. Indeed, major fashion groups such as Arcadia, which include Topshop, Dorothy Perkins and BHS, are looking at store closures in the UK, while others such as M&S, Debenhams and John Lewis are beefing up what they call their multi-channel strategies. Ideas such as 'click and collect', where shoppers can order online and then pick goods up from in store, or at a local post office, and 'quick response' (QR) labels which can be scanned with a smart phone that take shoppers straight to an online store, are all on trial. Some chains have even resorted to giving their store staff tablet computers, so they are better prepared to answer questions from their well-informed customers who have access to a wealth of information via their own phones.

In one of my own sectors, DIY, just six per cent of sales are currently online, but I can see that changing at a breathtaking rate already. Customers are becoming increasingly ready to order tools and paint online for next day, or even same day, delivery. Market leader B&Q is investing heavily in Internet and multi-channel services and I predict we will see a huge shake up in this sector in the next few years.

The inescapable fact is: many large retailers are still too slow to react to the current advances in technology. Take, for example, the current buzzword m-commerce, which I outlined a little earlier. Research has found that only five out of the UK's top 100 retailers have a mobile optimised version of their website[102] and the opportunities for social shopping experiences via websites like Facebook, were being virtually ignored. Although 65 per cent of these top chains could boast a Facebook 'fan' page, only four per cent went the extra mile to offer an

[101] Verdict
[102] One iota

integrated shopping function with it too. Yet, as history has shown, if the existing stores do not keep up, newer ones will be ready to take their place.

Many chains are still very vulnerable to competition from the Internet and I would be very surprised if some quite major names such as HMV and even Argos are still around in a decade's time. Many other smaller shops will continue to close too, thanks to pressure from the online environment.

Even those major retailers who have well and truly woken up to the threats and opportunities presented by the Internet, and who have carefully thought through a multi-channel strategy can't stop there though. The point about technology as I have illustrated here, is it keeps moving at a relentless pace. If bricks and mortar chains don't want to be left gaping like Catweazle, they need to think ahead and predict where it all might go next. Those that want to survive need to do a great deal of blue sky thinking and fast. Just as we used to do at Tesco in Lord MacLaurin's era, retail managers need to look ahead ten, or even 20 years or more, and imagine what issues will affect their business then. We already know about the Internet and m-commerce and the threat these technologies present, but what retailers need to do is to ask themselves what is on the horizon. If the sky was the limit, what could technology possibly conjure up? What is it that consumers most want to see? It is only by doing this that those retailers that are around today, will be able to survive in some shape or form, into the decades ahead.

The elements that are most likely to shape which technologies succeed in the future and which fails are many-fold. While this book has painted a gloomy future for the High Street, bricks and mortar stores will not disappear altogether. Many, many more casualties are expected, but even though online shopping will continue to grow, customers will still visit at least some stores in the future as part of a rich retail experience. It is, however, likely that they will favour large retail centres and malls, which can offer so much more, rather than their more down-at-heel retail cousins on the High Street. There will be a demand for more retailtainment – which is a combination of retail and entertainment, or a fuller shopping experience if you will, where shops are partnered with restaurants and leisure experiences such as bowling and cinemas. Those High Streets, secondary malls and out-of-town parks that cannot offer these things will eventually disappear.

Ironically, looking to the future and embracing technology may actually hold the key to giving customers that added extra, the personal service from years gone by which was eased out by our obsession with price. Part of the reason why the concept of customer experience will become an increasing influence upon where people choose to spend their money is because price cannot continue to be the only battle-ground. There is only ever so low that any retailer can go, however slick and efficient they are, so at some point the pendulum will swing back towards customer service. It will, however, be the modern take on customer service, and how retailers interpret this in the future will probably be a million miles away from what my mum Louie enjoyed.

Computer giant Apple have already made some great inroads here and have made some extraordinary advances in the whole idea of customer experience. Their airy and attractive stores project a carefree and casual atmosphere, where consumers are actively encouraged to try out products. Apple sales associates have an unusual sales philosophy in that they are instructed not to sell, but rather solve customer problems. They have no sales quotas and receive no sales commission, because the brand's view is that people don't want to be *sold* to, or *buy* computers, they want to know what they can *do* with them. And it works.

Shoppers' expectations of retail experiences like this will grow. Those retailers that can offer something like Apple, or even better, or at the very least a seamless, multi-channel experience, merging their store, online and mobile shopping operations into a complete brand, will do better than those that don't.

It also can't be forgotten that the other huge opportunity presented by technology, and the Internet in particular, is that there are now fewer physical, technological or geographical barriers to our shopping experience. UK retailers will be able to attract shoppers from markets abroad, although they will also have to cope with the flip side of this, which is consumers will be free to roam the world in the search for a bargain.

But, with our crystal ball to hand, what else might we see in the retail future? Let's end this chapter with a bit of blue sky thinking as to what our shopping experience might be like going forward.

We are already close to the time when there will be no longer any need to queue at checkouts, before laboriously unloading our trolleys or baskets and then loading the products back into trolleys once they have been scanned. There is technology available that can scan goods as we put them in our trolleys and we'll be able to walk out of the shop by simply swiping our finally tally with our mobile phones.

Another innovation which is just around the corner is smart signage which will recognise that you have bought something before and will make you a personalised offer as you walk by.

Scientists are even experimenting with hologram greeters, to boost first impression of stores, and prototypes were deployed at the London 2012 Olympics.

Further into the future, let's say by 2050, it will be increasingly about the shopping experience coming direct to the individual consumer. In the home, smart, barcode enabled fridges and larders will be able to order food and drink for themselves, when supplies are getting low, taking the drudgery away from the consumer altogether. It doesn't matter if you are not in when it all arrives either – modern houses will all have one metre wide, fully refrigerated, outside mailboxes.

When clothing is ordered online, a virtual scanner system will be used by the consumer's home computer system, to ensure an exact fit to their body shape. Goods will arrive just hours after they are ordered, delivered by a driverless electric postal truck.

If, however, the shopper chooses to go to one of the major shopping malls, the experience will be chalk and cheese to what you might expect today. Shops will not be laid out how we have come to know them, with rows of clothes or household goods, neatly set out on shelves, sorted by colour or style. In fact, there may not be rows of physical products at all. Instead, shoppers could be shown into individual booths where they will be shown half-hour holographic fashion shows of product lines selected especially for them. The shops will have stored all of our details and can get all the rest of the information they need about us online.

Even a trip to the local pharmacy to ask for advice will no longer be the same. By then, consumers will be able to do their own weekly online digital health check, using hand-held scanners which they can run over their bodies to check for signs of illness. After the results are analysed by a remote health network, which will compare the data with millions of others worldwide, the most appropriate medicine will be automatically dispatched for same day delivery.

The first virtual telepathy devices will be making an appearance around now, which will enable people to communicate without computers or phones at all. The technology would have been getting better and better in the run up to 2050, starting off with headsets, visors and glasses, which enable consumers to directly link themselves into the World Wide Web to do their shopping in the virtual world, but by this time it is quite likely that the devices can be completely miniaturised and even fully implantable. Imagine – you think of the TV you really would like to buy and then just do it with a nod of your head!

All of this is possible and more. Indeed, early tests of the technology that is needed to make many of these things happen is already well under way. Which of the ideas catches on, and which don't is really in the lap of the consumer who will continue to provide the pressure for change.

You may have your own ideas on what their shopping experiences will be like in the future and for the generations to come. Who knows what the future will hold, but it is exciting to imagine the possibilities. One thing is certain though; the retail environment will continue to change and it will do so at a tremendous pace with all sorts of new Catweazle-style elec trickery to come!

Chapter Eleven
Re-stocking our High Streets

Apart from a few densely populated affluent locations, the High Street as a retail destination cannot be saved or recreated. It must evolve into a community centre that reflects the needs of a society, which is both demanding for convenience and aging in profile.

L ike it or not the bustling, busy High Street that I remember so fondly from my youthful shopping trips with my mother, Louie, is dead and cannot be revived. It simply cannot survive in its traditional format and the fact that one shop has closed after another bears testament to this fact.

We should perhaps give our traditional High Streets some credit for the fact they have lasted so long. Their newer cousins, the secondary shopping malls and out-of-town shopping parks that mushroomed in the late eighties and early nineties, will be gone in the blink of an eye in comparison. There are already signs of this rapid demise everywhere as shoppers desert these smaller sites in droves, succumbing to the siren call of newer, better, more lavish malls, or simply stay at home and shop on the Internet.

This trend, and the others identified throughout this book, is not going to change. No one is going to wave a magic wand and send us all scuttling back to the High Street, shopping baskets in hand. We, the consumer, like things the way they are. We like the convenience of large supermarkets, with everything under one roof, from eggs to entertainment and everything else in between. We like the fact that there is always a large free car park at our malls and superstores. We like the fact that we can do our food shopping twenty-four seven, but only need to do it once a week, or even fortnight, thanks to all the high-tech gizmos we've got at home. After all, who on earth has time any more to spend an hour a day or more shopping for their evening meal? We also like the fact that, at the flick of a switch, or click of a mouse more precisely, we can shop at stores anywhere in the UK, around the world even, and compare prices and deals, without ever leaving the house.

We, the consumer, have made our choice and have voted with our wallets.

It doesn't matter that hundreds of small shops have gone to the wall because they simply cannot compete in a marketplace where the lowest price has become King. That's not our problem, is it? It's this same attitude which means we can all justify to ourselves taking armfuls of free plastic bags every time we go shopping and then discard them without a second thought for the environment and our steadily filling landfill sites. Similarly, who really notices when these secondary malls and out-of-town sites empty out and become tumbleweed parks? No one gives a second thought to the fact that many of these sites are owned by pension giants such as Aviva, Hendersons and Standard Life, and if they keep closing at such a rate, it could have a catastrophic affect on all our futures. No, we don't care, because we are all living for today.

This might sound like a bleak, even negative, outlook, but it is an honest and frank appraisal of where we are today and it is high time we had some straight talking about the situation we are currently in.

The truth is, in all the soul searching about the future of our High Streets, all the exhortations to 'use it or lose it' and chintzy ideas about pop-up shops, market days and who knows what, we've all been missing the point.

No one wants the High Street anymore.

Yes, if you ask anyone of a certain age about the High Streets of their youth, they will get misty-eyed thinking about the traditional shops such as the butcher, baker and candlestick maker, and it is a lovely memory, but we have all moved on from that.

We have to accept that the High Street we remember is dying of a terminal illness. In fact, it is already dead in many towns and cities and it is never coming back. It is only by accepting this fact that we can start to do something meaningful about deciding what to do next.

This is not a retailing problem that can be 'solved' by the Government enlisting retail experts and commissioning reports such as the recent Portas Review. The £5.5 million Government package of support to help revive nearly 400 ailing High Streets, which was announced in July 2012 in response to that review, will not even scratch the surface of the problem. Nor will the so-called Portas Pilots, the 27-odd towns that have been earmarked for special attention from retail expert Mary Portas, the author of the report, as well as £100,000 to invest in their individual High Streets. To be blunt, it is all a waste of money and resources.

After all the money has been spent, the headlines written and the cameras have gone on to some other reality TV show, we will still have the same problem. Not enough people will shop at these stores, however glitzy the makeover. They all moved on long ago and the plain truth is they cannot be tempted back.

The High Street is no longer a retail issue. Quite simply, the plight of our High Streets is a national issue for society to understand and demand of its government appropriate actions. As such, we, the people, need to bring about a paradigm shift in thinking and accept that our society, lifestyle and values brought about the changes that I have experienced throughout my long career as a retailer. We can no longer turn a blind eye to this, either ignoring it altogether or blaming big retailers for getting us into this state, while carrying on regardless. Things need to change. And they need to change radically.

Everyone has to stop thinking about 'saving' the retail environment. No amount of lower rent periods, market stalls and pop-up shops is going to change the situation we have found ourselves in today. Apart from anything else, all the threats to the remaining High Streets that we still do have, are only going to accelerate. Technology will continue to evolve and change at a pace and people will gravitate more and more to large malls which offer so much more than mere shops. Online shopping will have an ever-growing impact on our buying experience and it is my contention that we are not that far from a time when 50 per cent of all non-food shopping will be done over the Internet. The percentage purchase of food over the Internet will not be far behind. We need to respond to all of this now.

So what of the future, once we accept as we have to that things are not going back? How can we find hope that we can respond to all of the issues highlighted in the previous chapters? As a community, we need a positive outlook to give us inspiration so that we can adapt our High Streets and threatened retail parks into productive areas for future generations. In order to do that, we must learn lessons from past experiences and face up to our contribution to the issues that we face. This is an essential process and has been the motivation for me to write this book.

Having now traced the development of retail over my 45-year career in the business, my own view is there is no one thing or event that we can point to and say it was that which caused the demise of the High Street. The erosion of our High Streets, secondary and out-of-town retail parks and the fall of numerous great retail brands is down to numerous factors. What unifies those factors though, is greed. Greed is the common thread that runs throughout this book.

- Greed by retailers to be bigger and better
- Greed by property developers who put down more retail space than was ever required
- Greed from private equity players, who extracted value out of store chains without improving the proposition
- Greed by individuals (some of whom have become rich beyond their wildest dreams) who have in some cases pressurised companies to a point of collapse in their quest for financial success
- Greed from the consumer to get more and more for less and less

Alongside this greed is a widespread lethargy to actually do anything about the situation we have found ourselves in. Here, the finger of blame must point firmly at successive governments who have either been so in thrall to big retail concerns that they have let them get away with things that are clearly against the public interest, or who have read situations so badly that they have made laughably bad policy decisions. In both cases the outcome is the same – the High Street suffers and nothing really changes. Nothing concrete has been done to stem the explosion of greed.

The High Street is not alone in being blighted by this greed. The global banking crisis which erupted in 2008, shows just how far we have sunk, while the subsequent astonishing revelations over phone hacking and the media just highlights that we have completely lost our way in terms of good old-fashioned morality and integrity.

This corrupted value system has played a big part in what has happened to our shopping environments. Retailers, property developers, councils, government and the general public have all demonstrated a consumer driven greed to have material items before they have been earned. This greed, coupled with our obsession for convenience as a "time poor community", has enabled retailers to develop the way they have.

We all need to redefine our values, with morals and ethics high on the agenda. Indeed, perhaps if bankers were rewarded for investing in things that directly improve the Gross Domestic Product (GDP), investing in innovation and industry that promotes productivity and for always telling the truth, then our world would immediately be a better place!

But, I digress. When I set out to write this book, I had no idea that I would conclude that the UK PLC is in desperate need of a "turnaround" approach that will galvanise the country into action and finally map out a proper and realistic future for our towns and communities. But, believe me, I know a turnaround situation when I see one.

All four of the major retail companies that I have led were in desperate need for a change in fortune when I took over. Indeed, three of those businesses; Wickes, The Big Food Group (Iceland, Booker and Woodwards) and Focus DIY, were effectively "bankrupt", where bank covenants had, or were about to be, breached, meaning that the banks could have called in the administrators to liquidate the assets to get their money back at any moment. In each case we were able to persuade them to provide us with time to improve the performance of the businesses and get their lending on a more secure footing. And, although Park 'n' Shop in Hong Kong was part of a major group, and not threatened by the banks, it too was in desperate need of a turn-around. My track record as leader of these major turnarounds is; two wins (Wickes and Park 'n' Shop), a score draw (The Big Food Group) and one defeat with Focus DIY. With the exception of Focus DIY, all of the other companies have not looked back and have gone on to bigger and better performances, which suggests that the foundations in each case, laid throughout the five-year turnaround, provided a solid platform from which to grow.

None of this is to blow my own trumpet, it is merely to illustrate the fact that anything is possible. Once you recognise the problem, admit what has led up to it and decide on a proper (and realistic) way forward, things can be bought back from the brink. Most of the time. This is not to say that we will be able to return to the days of the traditional High Street we nostalgically think about, because to reiterate, that is not possible. It is simply to say that, with the right vision and a plan, it will be possible to create new and rewarding focal points for our communities. Our town centres can thrive again – but in an entirely different form.

With the benefit of my own experiences of turnarounds, I have concluded that if we are to deal with the issues of the High Street, we as a nation need to define what success looks like in 20 years' time. The main reason why we have let the situation erode to such an extent is because not enough people have taken the time to do some real blue sky thinking about where we might be in 2030, 2040, or 2050, or beyond. What we need to talk about now is our "Picture of Perfection" a long way ahead.

In the past, if there is any thought given to this issue at all, it generally centres on short-term fillips to get people into their local shops. Where we go from there (even if we do somehow manage this) is not really on the agenda.

A lot of the blame for this must lie with the authorities who are, after all, elected to serve the best interests of the people. As I highlighted earlier, successive governments have failed to do anything meaningful about our town centres because they either don't see it as a pressing problem, or politicians are to busy pursuing party policy and other interests, to really do anything more meaningful than a few headline-grabbing pronouncements. Despite clear evidence that thousands of stores are closing and dozens of town centres are little more than boarded-up shells, which attract crime and antisocial behaviour, there appears to be no political will to tackle the problem for the long-term. Thus, if the issues are considered at all, the problems of our High Streets are viewed in five-year electoral terms and a five-year view is nowhere close to being long enough.

How would I kick things off, if it was left up to me? Well, one of the first things I have done in every turnaround situation is imagine what I would like people to be saying about my company in 20 years' time. If I could sum it up in one sentence, what would that sentence be? Thus for Wickes, my mission statement for the future was:

To become the leading retailer of home improvement products, first choice for keen DIYers and tradesmen and a great place to work.

Once we'd agreed it, we made it part of everything we did and every strategy was tested against our vision of where we wanted to be.

So, as a starter for ten, here is my mission statement for UK PLC, for 20 years hence:

In 2032, the UK is a prosperous, harmonious, safe, cosmopolitan community competing in the Global economy with full employment, excellent healthcare, top-rate education and is surprising the world with its industry and continuous innovation.

Leading the way for a sustainable future and having fun.

Having set the goal or mission, traditionally the next step is to create a plan, or road map, of how to get there. Once that is done, successful turnarounds then define a set of values and principle that govern the behaviour along the journey, which basically asks: "How will things get done around here?"

I've chosen to tackle those values and principles first in the case of my virtual plan for UK PLC, to help us better understand why we are where we are and what we need to change to achieve our mission. I have though also included a few suggestions as to how we might create a road map to achieve our goals.

For sake of clarity, I've broken the mission down and tackled some of the key parts individually with ideas of how to move forward. You may well have some ideas that you'd like to add, and that's great, but this is just to get the dialogue started.

Prosperous

This may be a grand aspiration, particularly in the light of the state of the economy today, but in many ways it is key to the entire vision. We as a nation need to resurrect the proud working class and get people working and producing, rather than coveting what people apparently better off than ourselves own. The riots in the summer of 2011, where more than half the recorded offences were for looting, often high value branded designer clothes, trainers and mobile phones, should have been a real wake-up call for the authorities.

The report by the Riots Communities and Victims Panel[103], which followed the widespread disturbances, concluded that the riots were fuelled by a range of factors including a lack of opportunities for young people, poor parenting and materialism. The main recommendations were "to have communities that work" and a youth job promise to get more young people into the workplace. Since then though, there has been very little evidence of any firm action.

To achieve this prosperity, we need to fix a great deal more than our ailing High Streets. Radical changes are required to address these issues and they are not likely to be addressed by a coalition government obsessed with the national deficit and austerity programmes that are suffocating our economy that needs stimulus and growth.

We have not alleviated any of the symptoms which led to the earlier community unrest. There is an underclass of young people out there who don't have jobs that, given the opportunity, will rise up once again. It really wouldn't take much to make it happen either and as we know, any disarray will spread like wildfire, thanks to social media. Unless we give some serious thought as to how we can get people into work, I fear for the future.

---

[103] http://riotspanel.independent.gov.uk/

Suggestions abound as to how this might be achieved, but supporting what is left of our manufacturing industry, as well as our legions of small and medium sized businesses, which are the lifeblood of the economy, sound like a good start to me. Encouraging more well-run apprentice schemes, where young people actually learn valuable skills, rather than just being used as a short-term spare pair of hands on spurious work experience schemes, would also benefit us all in the long run.

Harmonious and safe

There are no two ways about it, empty and boarded-up shops are eye-sores and crime magnets. They signal that the local economy is at rock bottom and become a hot spot for every kind of antisocial behaviour imaginable. They drag down the whole feel of an area and lead to a spiral of decline.

We need to find a use for our High Streets that will make use of this space, get people back into the town centres and make them a bustling, positive area to visit. If it is not retailers that will fill these empty units, what could it be?

I believe the key to this lies in the next key word of the vision: *community.*

Community

The UK's High Streets have a real opportunity here to become the focal point for communities once again, but just in a *different* way. Community is important and the need for it will be greater than ever in the years to come.

Why? The flip side to us all shopping on the Internet, communicating to our friends via online social networks and taking advantage of the plethora of digital entertainment opportunities at home, is there are less reasons than ever to go out, mix with our peers and socialise. Yet, as researchers have found, those who constantly browse the web on their computers for hours at a time leave themselves wide open to developing stress, sleeping disorders and depression[104].

---

[104] University of Gothenburg

The High Street is the obvious place to focus on all the things that can't be done online and any future plans should consider prioritising initiatives which involve the body or social self. This means restaurants, cafes, pedestrianised meeting areas, art galleries or advice centres. Anything in fact, that will entice people out of their homes and encourage them to interact with one another and enjoy each other's company in a mutually fulfilling way. Local councils could step in and encourage schemes that get these type of enterprises to fill the empty shops. This sort of initiative will have the twin advantages of getting people out of their homes into a social environment, while also preventing former retail premises from falling into disrepair and blighting our town centres.

Competing in the Global economy with full employment

One of the most glaring discrepancies which have come to light in researching and writing this book is the ever-widening North-South divide which has had a real impact on retailing. As I showed in chapter five, the average national vacancy rate – number of empty shops – is 14 per cent, but Northern towns make the top ten worst performers[105], with vacancy rates of 25 per cent or more, compared with less than nine per cent in the more affluent south. The variance is just as marked in the jobs market. Unemployment in the North rose by almost 100,000 in 2011/12[106] and the number of people out of a job for more than a year is also on the rise. The figures from the South-West and West Midlands continue to make bleak reading too.

As part of our long-term review of our towns and cities, we desperately need to give these areas greater local powers devolved from central government, to help them unlock their potential. There is a strong case for Special Economic Zones in the North-East and West, Midlands, South-West and South-East, to add to the existing Assembles in Scotland, Wales and Northern Ireland. These SEZs could be led by local teams that understand the issues and are charged with responsibility of getting our youth back to work. Whether it is getting stuff out of the ground, making products for the home and overseas markets, growing things, or re-building the infrastructure, this is what we should be

---

[105] Local Data Company
[106] IPPR

prioritising. Areas like this don't need window dressing. They need real meaningful action.

These local teams could easily be funded by central government through cutting out wasteful exercises. They would be responsible for co-ordinating local councils ensuring that "red tape" is eliminated in order to generate prosperous activity. Part of their remit would be to ensure that local councils address the High Street and get them used for the benefit of the community.

Excellent healthcare

When planning for the future of our urban spaces, there is another important trend that we have to consider. The UK has an ageing population and the number of people over the age of 85 is expected to more than double from 1.4 million now, to 3.5 million within 25 years.[107] That will present challenges to our already hard-pressed, under-resourced National Health Service. The need for healthcare services will disproportionally increase too, as senior citizens seek to take advantage of the expanding array of new technologies and treatments for managing illnesses and promoting active lifestyles. Outdated, redundant out-of-town shopping centres could become massive medical centres with all disciplines; doctors, dentists, opticians, physiotherapists, gymnasium and dance areas.

The debate still rages about how we might pay for the healthcare needs of our ageing population and I don't profess to have the answers here, but in terms of addressing the need for more physical premises to look after and treat the elderly, it seems to me that the High Street holds at least some of the answers. The obvious solution is to convert some of the retail premises that no one wants or uses, into healthcare venues that everyone needs and wants. The economics of this will, of course, be an issue, but once again unless we begin the debate, there is little chance we will get anywhere.

---

[107] Office for National Statistics

Top rate education

The rapidly rising number of children means there is a chronic shortage of primary school places and very often the existing provision is executed in buildings that are well below an acceptable standard. The coalition government has already made its views clear that it wants to encourage parents groups and charities to set up free schools and it seems obvious that, once again, our town centres offer a perfect solution.

There have already been several instances of empty shop units being converted into free schools and one firm, building consultancy EC Harris, estimates it would cost about £13m to £17m to create a school using an existing retail shell, which is a saving of around a third on starting a new build from scratch. The conversion process could take as little as 20 to 35 weeks, which is the fraction of the time of a new build too. Our hundreds of empty shops could be the foundation for an affordable means of providing much needed extra school space. If less is spent on premises too, more can be invested into the quality of education that future generations receive inside these new schools.

Continuous innovation

Here's a thought; why do we need commercial units on our High Streets at all? (Particularly when we have clearly outgrown them.) The UK has a serious housing shortage because successive governments have failed to build enough houses to meet demand, which in turn pushes house prices even further out of most people's reach. Research has found that between 1997 and 2011, there has been a 20 per cent increase in the number of 20 to 34 years olds living with their parents[108]. There are not enough homes to go around. Why, therefore, don't we convert some of our numerous empty shop units into affordable housing?

To do this, the Government would have to reform the cumbersome Classes Order planning system, which designates land and buildings for particular purposes. At present, to move a shop from one Class Order to, say, domestic use requires planning permission and is by no means always a done deal.

---

[108] Office for National Statistics

If the change-of-use rules were relaxed, it would prevent local councils trying to second guess the market by forcing buildings to remain designated for purposes which are clearly no longer viable, such as retailing. It would open the way for people to forget about worthy (yet misguided) aims such as maintaining the High Street as a town centre focal point and start solving what is a real social issue.

It is innovative solutions such as this that will transform our local communities and provide them with what they really need.

Sustainable future

In this bleak assessment of the High Street's future, it is important to note that shops will not disappear forever. Although there will be a great deal more consolidation, as shops gravitate to larger malls and even the grocery giants will inevitably begin to cull their space as shoppers increasingly turn to the Internet, shops will still exist.

Retail groups cannot be forgotten in our plan for 20 years hence and must be included in all the discussions. And, as we shape what our retail environment will look like in two decades' time, we must all give some thought to the wider environment. We can none of us continue to turn a blind eye to trends such as the overuse of plastic bags at the checkout. Both retailers and consumers must start taking responsibility for what they do to their planet. In fact, an outright ban on the use of plastic bags should be one of the first decisions enacted. It has been done elsewhere in the world, so why not in the UK? Alongside this, retailers must also ramp-up their activities in areas such as reducing waste and saving energy, with genuine initiatives.

Having fun

Whenever anyone talks about the High Streets they talk about boarded-up shops, empty units, the demise of a favourite independent shop and so on. Everyone it seems has a sad story to tell and it is all pretty depressing, negative stuff. It's time to turn that on its head and look forward to all the fun we can have in our town centres. Let's find a way to celebrate our common areas, bring the community together in a new way and embrace all the fun we can have there. It is time to change attitude!

A great place to start is with the general look and feel of our High Streets. So much of our town centre architecture is off-putting today. We've designed benches that you can't sleep on, doorways you can't hang out in and lit up every corner with a blinding fluorescent glow. Historically, the philosophy has all been about repelling the undesirable element who may litter up our town centres, but what it has done is mean they evolve to pretty foreboding areas.

It's time to turn this on its head and bring back the fun into our town centres. Landscape architects could be brought in to spruce them up, even make them into giant gardens or playgrounds. Add in a skateboard park or a BMX area and the young people will soon come back. Give older people somewhere comfortable to sit and chat, others places to lounge around and relax. You'd be amazed what a sense of community this simple interaction would bring.

And that, in a nutshell, is a vision for the future.

Some of these ideas may seem overly idealistic. Others might just be out of reach altogether because of the potential costs involved. But, all of these ideas still just touch the surface of what we could achieve in the next 20 years. My strongest hope is that they will at least inspire some sort of debate and take us away from the anxious soul searching about how we can restore our High Streets back into something nobody really wants.

There is no logic in attempting to revive our High Streets as shopping centres. Instead, we should all be concentrating our energies on working out new ways to use this space productively and restore it to being the centre of our communities. I firmly believe that with some imagination, along with a realignment of our morals, ethics, integrity and value systems we may be able find a way forward.

So, let's stop this talk of saving the High Street and begin a debate about the real issue at hand. If we get behind this now, this could be a spectacular turnaround that really will make UK PLC the envy of the world.

It's time to start making our High Streets a better place and a centre of our communities once again.

Lightning Source UK Ltd.
Milton Keynes UK
UKOW06f1937060316

269706UK00003B/21/P